D1083498

A History of
Evangelism In The United States

A History of Evangelism In The United States

By

W. L. MUNCY, JR.

Professor of Evangelism and Missions
Central Baptist Theological Seminary

Kansas City, Kansas
Central Seminary Press
1945

Printed by the
Central Seminary Press
Kansas City, Kansas
U. S. A.

DEDICATION

This volume is dedicated to Mr. A. L. Ernst, a faithful and
beloved deacon in the Savannah Avenue Baptist
Church of Saint Joseph, Missouri, whose
interest in evangelism has been an
inspiration to the author
through the years.

ACKNOWLEDGMENTS

The author desires to express his appreciation to the following persons and publishers who have kindly given permission to quote from their copyrighted works:

Harper and Brothers Publishers, New York, from *A History of the Expansion of Christianity*. Vol. IV.

The Macmillan Company, N. Y., from *Timothy Dwight, A Biography* by Cunningham.

The Americana Corporation, New York, from *The Encyclopedia Americana* Vol. 29

Duke University Press, Durham, N. C., from *The Great Awakening in Virginia* by Gewehr.

PREFACE

The complete story of evangelism in the United States can not be written. This work of redemption is primarily a work of the Holy Spirit, whose movements among men can not be fully comprehended nor adequately described by a finite mind. Many of the men and women who have been used of the Holy Spirit to win others to Christ have come from the ranks of the common people. Their records have not been written. Eternity alone will reveal the full worth of their work.

There have been great movements in evangelism in the life of our country from the founding of the Jamestown colony to the present. Vital religion has ebbed and flowed. These trends appear in clear outline and are described in some detail in this volume. Social and economic forces have definitely affected these trends and have been affected by evangelism. Great personalities have appeared and have made valuable contributions. Their work has been described and evaluated in the context of history. New methods and techniques have been evolved to meet new situations. Some have served their day and lost their effectiveness. Much space is given in this volume to the description and evaluation of these methods.

The contributions of vital evangelism to the life of our nation appear in all areas of life. Two separate chapters are given to summaries of these contributions and the final chapter is an effort to understand the day in which we live in the light of history.

The author is happy to acknowledge his indebtedness to Dr. E. F. Haight, Professor of Christian History in the Baptist Bible Institute of New Orleans, Louisiana, and to Dr. C. Penrose St. Amant, Professor of Theology in the same institution. Both of these men made valuable suggestions in personal interviews and letters when the author first conceived the idea of writing a history of evangelism. He is also indebted to Dr. H. E. Dana, President of Central Baptist Seminary of Kansas City, Kansas, and to Dr. Eric G. Haden, Professor of Religious Education in the same institution, for reading and criticising the manuscript and for making many valuable suggestions. Important suggestions have been made also by Dr. W. W. Sweet of the University of Chicago and Dr. Kenneth Scott Latourette of Yale. It was the author's privilege to have one personal interview with Dr. Sweet and an extensive correspondence with both of these outstanding scholars. He is grateful for the help they have given. Dr. Walter E. Woodbury, Director of Evangelism for the Home Mission Society of the Northern Baptist Convention, has helped through personal interviews and correspondence. His deep and abiding interest in the subject has been an inspiration to the author. Finally, the author is indebted to the students of Central Baptist Seminary for a sympathetic hearing of this story in the class room and to Miss Mildred Snell who has prepared the index. It has been taught twice as a lecture course while the manuscript was being prepared. The interest of the students has been a constant inspiration and their frank discussions have been very helpful.

The book is to be used as a textbook in Central Baptist Seminary, but the author trusts that it will be of value to the general reader. He feels that pastors, laymen and all Christian workers will find information and suggestions here which will help them to present Christ to this generation more effectively. If the book can be used to advance His sway over men the author will be grateful.

INTRODUCTION

In keeping with a relationship which has been true of so many developments in the New World, the roots of American evangelism strike back into the religious soil of Europe.

Three revival movements were related to the Great Awakening in Colonial America and made invaluable contributions. They were the Pietistic movement in Germany, a vital evangelical awakening in Ireland, and the Wesleyan revival in England.

The Pietistic movement came to Germany as a reaction against certain trends in the Lutheran Church. This State Church of Germany had drifted away from the original teaching of Luther that the Bible is the only authority for faith and life. Instead of the Word of God, the creedal statements of the Church were expounded from the pulpits as authoritative. This departure from the Bible had produced a meaningless formalism in worship and a belligerent attitude toward hereties and unbelievers. It had also produced a generation of church members who knew little or nothing of a vital, personal, religious experence.[1]

The Pietistic revival began in 1670 when Philip Jakob Spener, pastor of the Lutheran Church at Frankfurt, began to conduct private meetings in his own home.[2] This earnest pastor was alarmed over the conditions prevailing in the church and was convinced that a return to the Bible and to a vital conversion experience was imperative. The meetings in his home were attended by a few kindred spirits who studied the Scriptures devotionally and shared their religous experiences through their testimonies. They sought for progressive experience through prayer as well as devotional Bible study and testimony. Spener also repeated his ser-

1. *The Encyclapedia Americana,* Vol. 22. p. 78.
2. *The Encyclapaedia Britannica* Vol. 7. p. 919.

ix

mons of the previous Sunday in these informal meetings.
Spener published a book entitled Pia Desideria in 1675
in which he advocated: (I) an earnest study of the Scriptures in such private meetings as he had been conducting in
his home; (II) giving laymen a share in the government of
the Church; (III) insistence from the pulpit upon the necessity of a vital religious experience; (IV) persuasion rather than
invective in dealing with unbelievers; (V) making the seminaries schools of personal Christian growth as well as schools
of doctrine; and (VI) loving persuasion to faith and love
rather than tricks of rhetoric in the pulpit.

The book received enthusiastic response from the faithful few among the clergy and from a large number of laymen. A group of theological students in the University of
Leipzig in 1794 began a devotional study of the Scriptures as
Spener and his friends at Frankfurt had been doing. These
meetings grew in interest and influence so rapidly that the
university authorities suppressed them. The students left
Leipzig and enrolled in the University of Halle which had
been established that year by friends of the pietistic movement. The founders of the new university with its orphanage were Spener, August Herman, Francke and Christian
Thomasius. They were assisted by Paul Gerhardt, singer
and composer whose hymns were genuine folk poetry. His
reputation has persisted to the present time. He was described in 1927 as the greatest hymn writer since Luther.[4]
He was the author of many hymns which were powerful in
influencing men toward Christ in the pietistic revivals.

Spener died in 1705, and Francke assumed leadership of
the movement. Through their insistence upon a return to
the Bible in preaching, their teaching that a vital Christian
experience must be followed by a moral reformation and practical Christian service, and their use of the hymns of Gerhardt the pietists were used mightily to bring revival and
reformation to the Lutheran Church. The Moravian Church

3. Bacon, L. W., A History of American Christianity, The Christian Literature Co. New York, 1897. p. 239.
4. The Concordia Encyclopedia, The Concordia Publishing House, St. Louis, Missouri, 1927, p. 169.

—organized by Count Von Zinzendorf in 1727—was also a fruit of the pietistic movement.

The pietistic movement waned in Germany by the middle of the eighteenth century but it made an invaluable contribution to evangelism in Colonial America. The Moravians settled in the middle colonies bringing the zeal of pietism to that section. Theodore J. Frelinghuysen came directly from Halle to New Jersey with an evangelistic passion that swept over the middle colonies in the Great Awakening era. George Whitefield was also influenced by the pietists.

A revival movement in Ireland also made a vital contribution to the Great Awakening revivals in the American colonies. This movement was not as widespread and powerful as were Pietism and Wesleyanism but its influence in America was quite as great as either.

The revival in Ireland began in 1642 when a number of Scottish regiments were sent into Ulster as an army of occupation following the rebellion of 1641. The chaplains of these regiments were Presbyterians and so were most of the suppressed Protestants of Ulster. These chaplains led in "a great religious revival[5] which led to the organization of a presbytery within a few months. The first meeting of the new presbytery was held at Carrickfergus in June, 1642. Five years later, the presbytery was composed of thirty ordained ministers with fixed charges in addition to the chaplains. Within fifteen years there were seventy ministers, a general assembly and a hundred thousand members of Presbyterian churches in Ulster.

The unsettled political status of Ulster brought on persecution, but the Presbyterian ministers were allowed to resume their services in 1765. They were again suppressed and much of their property confiscated in 1782, but they had grown by that time to seventy-five ministers, one hundred congregations and five presbyteries.

The fortunes of another Protestant group, the Church of Ireland, were also changing in this era of political and religious strife. The outstanding leader of the Episcopal group

5. *The Encyclopaedia Britanica,* Vol. 22. p. 290.

was William King. He was educated at Trinity College, Dublin, and was made Bishop of Dublin in 1702. Through his influence the Church of Ireland was freed from the political domination of England and was committed to the task of ministering to the spiritual needs of the people.[6]

The evangelical doctrines, the evangelistic zeal and the church polity of the Presbyterians attracted many members of the Church of Ireland who became dissenters. A famous dissenter was William Tennent, a priest of the Church of Ireland. He migrated to New York and was received into a presbytery there in 1718. The Presbyterians received him without reordination upon his giving six reasons for dissenting. He was a preacher of "wondrous zeal"[7] and founder of the famous "Log College" at Neshaminy, Pennslyvania. In addition to his own evangelistic labors, Tennent inspired and trained many other evangelists of the Colonial period in America.

A third evangelistic movement in the Old World which influenced evangelism in Colonial America was the Wesleyan revival in England. It was contemporaneous with the Great Awakening era in America. For that reason its relationship to Pietism in Germany alone is traced here.

The private meetings of the pietists—begun by Spener—found reproduction in the "Holy Club" or "Methodists" in Oxford University in England. John and Charles Wesley were members of the society. The members of this group fasted twice a week, visited prisons and the sick, engaged frequently in prayer, meditation and self-examination in a quest for personal piety.[8] This was a regular technique of the Pietists and the Moravians.[9]

The music of the Methodist revivals—the songs of John and Charles Wesley—were mighty in influencing men toward

6. *The Encyclopedia Brittanica*, Vol. 15. p. 804.
7. Maxson, C. H., *The Great Awakening in the Middle Colonies*, The University of Chicago Press, Chicago, Ill. 1920. pp. 25-26.
8. *The Encyclopedia Americania*, Vol. 29. p. 296.
9. Luccacia, H. E. and Huachison, Paul, *The Story of Methodism*. The *Methodist Book Concern*, New York. 1926. pp. 56-60.

Christ just as the songs of Paul Gerhardt had been in Germany. The insistence of the Methodists upon a vital personal conversion experience, moral reformation and lives of practical service was also similar to pietist teachings. The earliest Methodist leaders had frequent fellowship with the Moravians. When John Wesley made his first trip to Georgia he brought a company of Moravians with him.[8]

The Methodist revival movement was in its beginnings in England when the Great Awakening came to America. George Whitefield came directly from that evangelistic movement to the colonies where he preached with great power and effectiveness. The first preachers to be sent to America by Wesley arrived in the colony of Virginia only a few years before the outbreak of the American Revolution but they were earnest and powerful evangelists.

CONTENTS

PERCENTAGES OF CHURCH MEMBERS

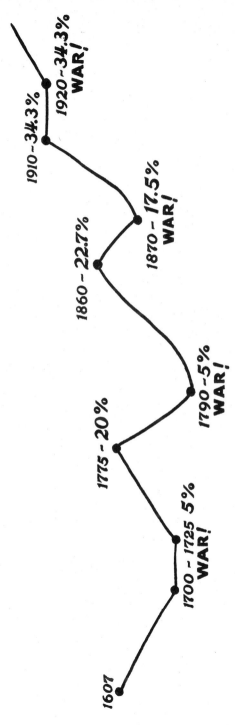

1607

1700 – 1725 **WAR!**

1725 5%

1775 – 20%

1790 – 5% **WAR!**

1860 – 22.7%

1870 – 17.5% **WAR!**

1910 – 34.3%

1920 – 34.3% **WAR!**

Percentages are in Ratio to total population in the United States, except 1725 which is in Virginia only. The 20% in 1775 is only an estimate

DIVISION ONE

THE PERIOD OF COLONIAL DEVELOPMENT

1607 - 1775

PART I
THE EARLY COLONIAL PERIOD
1607 TO 1700

CHAPTER I

A ZEAL THAT WANED

Every Christian group that came to the New World with the colonists was possessed with an earnest desire to Christianize the Indians as well as the settlers. The plight of the Red Man in his paganism and the needs of the colonists in the wilderness of America aroused the Christian compassion of many people in England and upon the Continent.

Alexander Whitaker, a gifted young clergyman, left a comfortable parish in England "to help bear the name of God unto the Gentiles" in Virginia. Nicholas Ferrar, Sr., a merchant in London, bequeathed twenty-four pounds "to be distributed to three discreet and godly men in the colony [of Virginia] which shall honestly bring up three of the Infidels' [the Virginia Indians'] children in the Christian religion and some good course to live by."[1] When a charter was granted to the Virginia Company, King James I directed that the Church of England was to be maintained in the New World and that it was to use all proper means "to draw the natives to the true knowledge and love of God." Clergymen in London preached to those who were about to sail for America about their responsibility for the Indians. On February 21, 1607, the Reverend William Crenshaw preached to Lord De la Warr and the Virginia Council just as they were about to set sail to assume control of the struggling colony on the James river. He said:

"Look not to the gaine, the wealth, the honor, but looke at those high and better ends that concerne the Kingdom of God. Remember thou art a General of Christian men, therefore, look principally to religion. You goe to commend it to

1. Tiffany, C. C., *A History of the Protestant Episcopal Church in the United States of America*, New York, Chas. Scribner's Sons, 1903, p. 22.

3

the heathen; then pratice it yourself; make the name of Christ honorable, not hateful to them."[2]

It is probable that the missionary work of the Catholics of Spain among American Indians had challenged Protestant England. At any rate, both England and continental Europe showed concern for Christianizing the aborigines of America.

I

The Church of England in Virginia

Inspired by the instructions of the King and the interest of their brethren in the mother country, the group that settled at Jamestown, Virginia, brought with them Robert Hunt, a faithful clergyman. Worship was instituted as soon as the colonists landed in 1607. A piece of the sail of the ship was stretched between two trees to afford shelter. A board was nailed to two trees to serve as a pulpit and the first Protestant religious service upon American soil was conducted by the Reverend Hunt.

The best known Anglican clergyman of this period, however, was Alexander Whitaker, who succeeded Hunt. He won Pocahontas to Christ and baptized her. This Indian princess was the first fruit of Protestant Christianity in America. The work of Mr. Whitaker won for him the title, "The Apostle to the Indians."

In 1613 Whitaker published a pamphlet in which he appealed for men and money to be used in Christianizing the Indians. This pamphlet was circulated in London where it aroused much interest. A few years later Pocahontas visited England with her husband, John Rolfe. Her presence increased the interest on the part of the Church of England. A group of Indian youth went to Britain to be educated, and their contacts with Christians further stimulated their concern for the Red Man on this side of the Atlantic.

A movement was soon started in London to raise funds to establish a university at Henrico, Virginia, for the Christian education of the Indians. Other schools were contemplated to

2. Tiffany, op. cit. p. 15.

become feeders for the university. The motive of this movement was a desire to bring the blessings of the Gospel to the natives.

But this enthusiasm which made such noble beginnings during the first fifteen years of the Jamestown colony had almost disappeared by the close of the century. Not more than one in twenty of the citizens of Virginia was a member of the Church in 1700. The lower classes were neglected almost entirely, having practically no interest in religion.

Many causes contributed to this loss of enthusiasm. The massacre of 1622 stopped the movement to build the university at Henrico. Seventeen workmen on the college grounds were murdered. Plans for other schools were also abandoned and the Christian concern for the Indians was supplanted by the spirit of hate, suspicion, and revenge.

The incompetence and, in some cases, the immorality of the clergy during the last half of the century produced further unconcern for the religious welfare of both the whites and the Indians. This condition was brought about, in some measure, by the fact that the control of the local churches was in the hands of the vestry. The Bishop of London was to "watch over" the infant Church of America, but the distance and the difficulties of communication made his oversight ineffective. The vestries often substituted "Lay readers" for ordained clergymen because they could be had at less expense. The tenure of the minister was so uncertain that his work was greatly hampered.

The lethargy of the Mother Church of England was reflected in the Church in Virginia. Civil war in Britain also disturbed the colony and accelerated the downward trend of religion and morals.

These forces operating on both sides of the Atlantic quenched the splendid missionary enthusiasm which would have built a university for the Christian education of Indian youth at Henrico and which would have provided for the spiritual welfare of the colonists. We shall see that a similar trend appeared in the life and work of the other Christian groups during the early Colonial Period.

II.

The Congregational Church in New England

The first Christian groups to settle in New England became the Congregational Church of America. The story of
the development of their church polity is very interesting but
it does not concern us here.

The Congregationalists had a vital interest in genuine
evangelism. They became Separatists only when they des-
spaired of purifying the Church of England. During the early
Colonial period they demanded evidence of regeneration as a
prerequisite to church membership.[3] If any one desired to
unite with the church he presented his request to the elders
who brought the matter to the attention of the congregation.
The procedure was followed in receiving male members, but
women were permitted to tell their experiences to the elders
only. When John Cotton joined the church at Boston, he related his experience to the congregation but his wife was received by the profession she made to the elders.[4]

The early Congregational ministers of New England bore
the cross in their attitude toward the unsaved. In an argument against the theory of Apostolic succession, which taught
that every minister must be consecrated by a bishop, an early
Congregational leader said:

"When we see a man called to the ministry by the Church
of God, his mind instinct with the grand truths of revelation, mighty in the Scriptures, fervent in spirit, instant in
prayer, BURNING WITH LOVE TO JESUS, AND TO
THE SOULS FOR WHICH JESUS BLED, laboriously and
faithfully dispensing the bread of life to hearts hungering for
the heavenly food, where is he who will coldly ask to see his

3. Dexter, Henry Martin, *The Congregationalism of the Last Three
Hundred Years,* New York, Harper, 1880, pp. 415, 445, 450, 460.

4. McClure, A. W., *The Life of John Cotton,* Boston, The Sabbath
School Society, 1846, p. 108,

ᴊommission to preach the Gospel, to ascertain if he is endorsed by human sanctions?"[5] This statement implies that the men who entered the ministry had a Christ-like passion for the lost. No specific examples are cited but the statement is general.

Church attendance was almost universal in the early New England settlements. It is well known that the governor, Captain Miles Standish, and other officials marched to church at Plymouth each Lord's Day to the beat of drums. They were followed by the entire population of the colony. This condition gave great evangelistic opportunity to the ministers who were "burning with love to Jesus and to souls for which Jesus bled." Since the sermon was the "main element" in their worship[6] the winning of men to Christ was to be expected.

The first and second groups of immigrants that followed the Pilgrims to New England presented a challenge to aggressive evangelism in the church. It is said of them that they were "rough enough" and that "some immigrants were so bad, as they were faine to be at charge to send them home the next year".[7] The Virginia Company sent out such young men to New England because their interests were commercial. Whereas, the Pilgrims earnestly desired that Pastor Robinson and the rest of their group in Holland be allowed to come to the New World.

This challange was accepted by such men as Elder Brewster at Plymouth and John Cotton of Boston. Of Elder Brewster's ministry it was said that he, "Taught twice every Saboth and yt both powerfully and profitably, to ye great contentment of ye hearers and their comfortable edification; yea, and many were brought to God by his ministrie".[8] In spite of the fact that Mr. Cotton was much occupied in doctrinal discussions, his biographer relates that, "His labors in the pulpit and elsewhere were exceedingly great; and the power

5. *Ibid.*, p. 151.
6. **Sweet, W. W.,** *The Story of Religions in America,* New York. Harper and Bros., 1930, p. 81.
7. Walker, W., ,A *History of the Congregational Churches in the United States,* New York, Chas. Scribner's Sons, 1902, p. 69.
8. *Ibid.,* p. 73.

of God mightily attended them, and crowned them to the conversion of numerous souls, and the edification of thousands".[9]

The Church under the leadership of such men as Brewster and Cotton was the social and political center of the community. It grew to such proportions that it was the predominating influence in four colonies in New England by 1650. Even though many immigrants were so bad that the leaders desired to deport them, the religious and moral conditions became so good that a New England minister could tell his friends in London that, "I have lived in a country where in seven years I never saw a beggar, heard an oath nor looked upon a drunkard".[10] These conditions bear testimony to the zeal and the effectiveness of early Congregationalists in winning men to Christ.

The second half of the century witnessed a sad decline in evangelism among the New England Congregationalists. Toward the close of the century William Brattle and William Leverett, tutors at Harvard and Cambridge, began to advocate certain changes. They argued that membership in the church should not depend upon the "relation" of a Christian experience before the congregation. Ministerial associations were formed in which debates arose over doctrines and polity. The question of the relationship between Church and State was also a subject of much acrimonious debate. Dr. W. W. Sweet says that, "The religion of the Puritans had become unemotional, with a type of preaching unconducive to revivals and conversion".[11]

Many forces operated to produce this condition. The adoption of the Half-way Covenant near the middle of the century had produced a generation of church members many of whom were unregenerate. The limiting of the franchise to church members had drawn others to the church for ulterior objectives. The disputes over doctrines, the relationship between Church and State, and church polity had occupied the time and the energies of many leaders. King Philip's War

9. McClure, op. cit., p. 251.
10. Ibid , p. 255.
11. Sweet, op. cit., p. 96.

and the political unrest which ensued greatly disturbed the colony and the severe persecution of the Quakers engendered a spirit which hindered the churches in winning men to Christ as they had done in the early years of the Colonies.

III.

The Quakers

The Quakers were one of the most influential groups in the evangelization of the Indians and the colonists in the beginnings of the American colonies. Their quest for a vital, personal religious experience is the first evidence of a genuine evangelism. They may have gone to extremes in their teaching about direct divine guidance in the individual soul, but this yearning for a vital touch with God is the fountain-head of their widespread evangelistic endeavors in the wilds of Colonial America.

The missionary undertakings of this humble group touched many lands. They were persecuted, but this fact did not deter them. George Fox, the founder of the movement, was imprisoned more than sixty times covering a period of eleven years in England. The first Quaker missionaries to America were two women, and they were denied the privilege of disembarking from their ship in Boston. After being permitted to land they were imprisoned for five weeks. Boards were nailed over the windows of their jail to prevent them from speaking to people on the outside and their books were burned. They were examined for evidences of witchcraft and deported. Subsequently, many laws were passed in Massachusetts to suppress the Quakers.

In spite of this persecution—or more likely because of it—the Friends grew rapidly in all the earliest colonies. At the close of the seventeenth century there were forty meetings or congregations in Pennsylvania alone, and by the middle of the eighteenth century their adherents numbered thirty thousand.

In 1671 George Fox, accompanied by twelve other missionaries, came to America and spent two years in the Colonies. Fox preached in New England, New Jersey, Delaware,

Maryland, and Carolina. The other missionaries served with him and under his direction. The hardships they endured for the Gospel's sake remind one of the life and labors of the Apostle Paul.

The personal Journal of George Fox reveals something of the methods employed by these itinerant evangelists. He also records the results of their labor with glowing enthusiasm and sincere praise. Of their first meeting in the New World, in the colony of Maryland, he writes:

"A very large meeting was held four days, to which (besides Friends) came many of the world's people, divers of whom were of considerable quality in the world's account. After the public meetings were over, the men's and women's meetings began, wherein I opened to the Friends the service thereof to their great satisfaction."[12]

Following this initial meeting the thirteen missionaries were divided into four groups to visit other colonies and to conduct meetings similar to this one. Such a meeting, held at Flushing, New York, is described by Mr. Fox as follows:

"The half-year's meeting began next day, which was the first day of the week, and lasted four days. The first and second days, we held public meetings for worship, to which the people of the world of all sorts might, and did come; on the third day of the week were the men's and women's meetings, wherein the affairs of the Church were taken care of. Here we met with some of the bad spirits, who were run out from truth into prejudice, contention, and opposition to the order of truth and to Friends therein. These had been very troublesome to Friends in their meetings there and thereabouts formerly, and, it is like, would have been so now; but I would not suffer the service of our men's and women's meetings to be interrupted and hindered by their evils. Wherefore, I let them know, that if they had anything to object against the order of truth which we were in, we would give them a meeting on another day on purpose. And, indeed, I labored the more, and traveled the harder, to get to this meeting, where

12. Fox, George, *Passages from the Life and Writings of George Fox,* Philadelphia, The Friends Book Store, 1801, p. 262.

it was expected many of these contentious people would be, because I understood they had reflected much upon me when I was far from them.   So, the men's and women's meetings being over, on the fourth day we had a meeting with these discontented people to which as many of them as would, did come, and as many Friends as had a desire were present also; and the Lord's power broke forth gloriously, to the confounding of the gainsayers.   And then some of them that had been chief in the mischievous work of contention and opposition against the truth began to fawn upon me, and to cast the matter upon others; but the deceitful spirit was judged down and condemned, and the glorious truth of God was exalted and set over all, and they were all brought down and bowed under, which was of great service to truth, and great satisfaction and comfort to Friends.   Glory to the Lord forever!"[13]

These methods—public meetings for preaching to the unconverted as well as to the Friends, private meetings with the churches for instruction, counsel, and discipline, and personal testimony—bore a rich harvest.   Even the avowed enemies of the Friends were won.

After two years of such labor in America, Fox felt that his "spirit was free" in regard to the New World.   He returned to England and to other fields of service.   The Friends lost their evangelistic zeal for the unsaved almost entirely by the end of the seventeenth century.   Dr. W. W. Sweet says, "but as numbers increased spiritual life seemed to decline"[14] by 1700.   In the early eighteenth century, itinerant Quaker preachers spoke of "a dry and lifeless state" among their churches.

The reasons for this loss of missionary and evangelistic fervor are quite obvious.   The adoption of "Birthright Membership" about the middle of the century bore fruit in an unregenerated membership by the close of the century.   A similar condition obtained among the Congregational churches in New England as a result of the Half-way Covenant.   Unregenerate people have no missionary compassion.

13. Fox, op. cit., p. 264-265.
14. Sweet, op. cit., p. 147.

The disappearance of persecution contributed to this state of apathy. Like many other Christian groups, the Quakers "went everywhere preaching the Word" and winning men when persecution was rife. But when it was easier to be a Christian this earnestness and faithfulness were not in evidence.

Increasing wealth and worldliness also helped to quench the fires of missionary and evangelistic work by the close of this century. An aged Friend, looking back over some sixty years, wrote in 1760:

"Friends were a plain lowly-minded people, and there was much tenderness and contrition in their meetings. That at 20 years from that date, the Society increasing in wealth and in some degree conforming to the fashions of the world, true humility was less apparent, and their meetings not so lively and edifying. . . . Powerful overshadowings of the Holy Ghost were less manifest in the Society".[15]

Thus the spirit of evangelism flowed and ebbed in the Society of Friends. Their zeal swept over all of the colonies and won many people to Christ in spite of persecution and hardship during the first twenty-five years of their activities in the New World. But the second quarter of a century witnessed a sad decline for the reasons mentioned above.

IV.

Dutch Reformed and Swedish Lutherans

Two religious groups appeared early in New Amsterdam and New Jersey to play a vital role in the evangelization of the settlers and the Indians. But for the changing political fortunes of the colony they would likely have grown to be large and influential denominations in America. They were the Dutch Reformed Church, the State Church of the Netherlands, and the Swedish Lutherans.

The Dutch Reformed Church had its beginning in the New World in New Amsterdam in 1638—five years after the founding of the colony. Rev. Jonas Michaelius was the

15. *Ibid.*, p. 147.

first minister. At the first communion service in the new church, many were received upon the testimony of their friends to the fact that they were members of the church in the mother country. Michaelius says that some had forgotten their Church certificates, some had lost them, and others did not bring them to the New World because they did not suppose that a church would be established there. This minister served the Dutch settlers and the French Walloons, administering the Lord's Supper to the latter group in the French language. This first Dutch Reformed minister remained in America only a few years.

Under the "Patroon" system several Dutch ministers came to the colony. The best known of this group is John Van Mecklenburg. The claim has been made that he was the first Protestant missionary to the Indians. He learned the Mohawk language, preached to this tribe in their own tongue, and won converts. The Indian converts were received into the Dutch churches rather than being organized into separate congregations.

When the English captured New Amsterdam in 1664, there were six Dutch ministers and thirteen churches in the colony.

Swedish Lutheran settlers appeared on the Delaware river in 1638 and established a colony. They built a fort which was called "Fort Christiana". Reverend Reorus Torkillus was with this group. He was the first Lutheran minister to come to the New World. He died in 1643 and was succeeded by Reverend John Companius.

It is said of Companius that, "He ministered faithfully to the settlers and undertook the Christianizing of the Indians in the vicinity."[16] New Sweden was captured by the Dutch in 1655, and the Dutch colony was taken over by the English in 1664. The Swedish Lutherans had made a good beginning in evangelizing the settlers and the Indians. Two churches remain to this day—the Gloria Dei Church in South Philadelphia and the Old Swedes Church in Wilmington, Delaware—as a testimony to their work in the early Colonial period.

16. *Ibid.*, p. 131.

CHAPTER II

TRIUMPH AND TRAGEDY IN INDIAN EVANGELIZATION

It was noted in chapter one that all the religious groups among the colonists made some effort to Christianize the Indians. The Church of England made a good beginning in Virginia in the early years of the seventeenth century. George Fox, the founder of the Society of Friends, preached to American Indians and won converts. Both the Dutch Reformed and the Swedish Lutherans preached to the Red Men and were successful in winning some of them to Christ. Roger Williams and John Clark, Baptist ministers, did extensive mission work among the Indians which greatly influenced them in their attitudes toward the white man. But the major Protestant effort to Christianize the original Americans was made by the Congregational church in New England—a movement sponsored by the government and the Church of the Standing Order.

In 1646 the General Court of Massachusetts passed the first act encouraging the propagation of the gospel among the Indians, and recommending to the elders of the churches to consider the means by which it might be effected. The work was begun the same year by the Reverend John Eliot, pastor at Roxbury.

Eliot learned the language of the natives and then arranged to preach to a group of them about five miles from his home. Taking two or three friends with him, he approached the appointed place and was met by Chief Waban and a number of his braves. The Chief and his attendants escorted the company to a large wigwam where a crowd had gathered to hear the new doctrine. Eliot's sermon covered, "most of the articles of Natural and Revealed Religion".[1]

"HE SPOKE OF THE CREATION of the world, the fall of man; the greatness of God, the Maker of all things; of

1. Brown, William, *History of Christian Missions*. London, T. Baker. 1864, v. 3 p. 32.

14

the Ten Commandments, and the thunderings denounced against the transgressions of them; of the Character and Office of Jesus Christ; of the last Judgment, the joys of heaven and the terrors of hell."[2]

Following the sermon, which lasted one hour, an open forum was held, the Indians asked questions and Eliot sought to answer them in plain and simple language. It is said that, "The Indians not only listened to him with great attention, but some of them appeared deeply affected by what they heard."[3] Eliot suggested to the General Court that a grant of land for an Indian Village be made. This was done in 1636 and the first village of "Praying Indians" was built. They named it Nooantomen, which means "Rejoicing". This became a custom. Many villages were built for Indian converts that they might be free from persecution of their people who opposed the gospel and that they might have opportunity to develop a Christian civilization.

Eliot continued as pastor of the Roxbury Church, but visited the Indians twice each month. He preached to them and conducted the forum following each sermon. Many were the hardships which this first missionary to the Indians endured. He wrote to a friend, "I have not been dry night nor day from the third day of the week to the sixth, but have travelled from place to place in that condition; and at night I pull off my boots, wring my stockings, and on with them again and so continue."[4] Indian chiefs and the priests alike were opposed to the gospel. They persecuted their countrymen who became Christians and even threatened the life of the missionary. In spite of such hardships, Eliot travelled over most of Massachusetts, preaching the Word to his Indian neighbors.

The evangelist made the gospel attractive to his hearers by the life he lived among them. He won their love and respect by many deeds of kindness. He always took his own provisions with him on his journeys and some small gifts for

2. *Ibid.*, p. 32-33.
3. *Ibid.*, p. 33.
4. *Ibid.*, p. 36.

the people. He often invited them to his own home where he served sumptuous meals. He refused to receive remuneration from them for his ministry because he thought in their poverty and their primitive state of culture, it would hinder the gospel to do so.

The first Indian church, the fruit of Eliot's labors, was organized at Natick, about eighteen miles from Boston, in 1660. Eliot invited the ministers from several neighboring churches to come together to hear the testimonies of the Indians. Having related their Christian experiences, several were baptized, admitted to the Lord's supper, and organized into a church. Their place of worship was a large room on the first floor of a two-story building in the center of the village.

As in all pioneer evangelism the printed page was used effectively among the Indians. Eliot's translation of the New Testament into the Indian tongue was published in 1661, and was to be followed two years later by his version of the Old Testament. This was the first Bible to be printed in America. Eliot also translated other Christian literature which was circulated among the Indians.

In the very beginnings of his work, Eliot sought to establish schools to educate Indian youth and to train native ministers. These schools were not as successful as their founders had hoped, but by 1674 many congregations in the fourteen villages of Praying Indians had pastors, elders and deacons of their own nation.

The work received a severe blow in 1675 when Philip, one of the principal chiefs, made war upon the English. Casualties were numerous on both sides. Enmity between the two races grew apace and many Indians renounced Christ. Others who remained faithful were killed. By 1684 there were only four places of worship, but services were conducted occasionally in other communities.

This tragic hindrance to the work was a heavy burden upon the aged minister who had given so many years of sacrificial service in preaching Christ to the Red Men. His advanced age prevented him from making the missionary journeys as frequently as had been his custom, but he was faithful to the very end of his life, making frequent preaching tours among them. During his last illness, he said:

"There is a dark cloud upon the work of the gospel among them. The Lord revive and prosper that work, and grant that it may live when I am dead. It is a work I have been doing much and long about. But, what was the word I spoke last? I recall that word, **My doing.** Alas! They have been poor, and small, and lean doings; and I will be the man who will throw the first stone at them."[5]

Having wrought heroically in the very spirit of Christ, the aged Apostle to the Indians went to his eternal reward on May twentieth, 1690, at the age of eighty-six.

The spread of the gospel among the Indians on the island of Martha's Vineyard was coincident with the movement in Massachusetts. In 1646, the year in which the work began in Massachusetts, the Spirit of God moved upon a chief whose tribe lived on this island to request that the gospel be preached to his people in their own language. He said to Thomas Mayhew, Sr., proprietor of the island, "Thou shalt be to us as one that stands by a running stream, filling many vessels; even so shalt thou fill us with everlasting knowledge."[6]

The interest of this chief had been aroused by the life and the testimony of the first native convert on the island. He was a young man by the name of Hiacoomes. He had been won to Christ by Thomas Mayhew, Jr., son of the governor of the island. Young Mayhew was located as pastor of the English group, but his zeal led him to extend his parish to include the Indians.

Mr. Mayhew's approach to the natives was wise and tactful. He sought "to win their affection by kind and gentle usage". The conversion of Hiacoomes was a result of this method. The young clergyman invited him to his home, entertained him in a very friendly manner and talked with him about the Christian religion. He soon renounced the religion

5. *Ibid.*, p. 42.
6. *Ibid.*, p. 47.

of his fathers and sought instruction from Mayhew. This aroused the natives and they persecuted the new convert without mercy. He remained constant and manifested the spirit of Christ in his attitude toward his persecutors. His constancy and his Christ-like attitude influenced the chief to request the gospel for his people.

The chief was opposed by some of his tribesmen, especially the Pawaws, or Priests. They often threatened the life of the missionary, but in 1650 two of the Pawaws were converted. Others followed and the persecution subsided.

Mayhew traveled extensively about Martha's Vineyard and the neighboring islands. He lived as the natives did, eating their food and sleeping in their wigwams. He catechized the children, preached to the people, and answered their questions in the open forum as Eliot was doing on the mainland. He also spent some time every Saturday helping young Hiacoomes to prepare sermons for his people. It was his custom to visit the Indians twice each month as Eliot did in Massachusetts.

The labors of this remarkable young man came to an untimely end in 1657. He sailed for England to present the cause of Indian evangelization to the churches of the mother country. The ship on which he was a passenger was lost at sea. No trace of the ship or of the voyagers was ever found.

Upon the tragic death of the illustrious son, Thomas Mayhew, Sr., took up the task of preaching Christ to the natives. At the age of seventy, he learned their language and, "though a governor, he was not ashamed to become a preacher among them".[7] The Indians soon asked the elder Mayhew to become their minister.

The ministry of the Mayhews and the two native pastors was so effective that by 1764 more than three-fourths of the three hundred native families on the Island were "Praying Indians". It is said that the elder Mayhew, despite his advanced age, often walked twenty miles through the woods to visit his Indian friends and to preach to them. He

7. *Ibid.*, p. 49.

often visited Nantucket, where in 1674 there was a church having thirty members in full communion, forty children who had been baptized, and about three hundred persons who prayed in their homes and observed the Sabbath.

Thomas Mayhew, Sr., governor of the Island, whose ministry began at seventy, died in 1680 at the age of ninety-three. He had given almost a quarter of a century of devoted service. He was succeeded by a grandson, John Mayhew, who was pastor of the English group at the time of his grandfather's death. His ministry was brief. He died at the age of thirty-seven, having been a preacher for sixteen years.

John Mayhew was succeeded as evangelist to the Indians by his eldest son, Experience Mayhew, in 1694. He was a master of the Indian language, having known it from infancy. He was employed to translate the Psalms and other portions of the Scriptures. By this time the Indian population had diminished to one hundred and eighty families, but only two persons among them continued in their ethnic faith. Thus the century closed with a fourth generation Mayhew witnessing for Christ and ministering to the natives on Martha's Vineyard and the other islands nearby.

PART II

THE LATER COLONIAL PERIOD

1700 - 1775

CHAPTER III

THE DARKNESS THAT PRECEDED THE DAWN

The half century from 1700 to 1775 may be described as the "dark age" for evangelism in Colonial America. The religious life in all of the colonies was in a decadent state. Consequently, immorality was rife and corruption in State and Church was alarming.

When Dr. Thomas Bray arrived in Maryland in 1700, as Commissary of the Church of England, he found such immorality among the clergy that it was necessary to discipline them. But when he called two of "the most flagrant offenders against morals and decency"[1] to account, both the clergy and the people were offended. Bray published A **Memorial upon the State of Religion in America** in which he appealed for "learned, strong and capable clergymen to become missionaries to America." He said that, "the refuse of the clergy in England" would not do for American missionaries. This zealous minister spent only a few months in Maryland but his ministry there revealed the tragic decadence of the Church of England in that colony. He returned to England where he died in 1734—the very year of the beginning in New England of the "Great Awakening" which was to sweep over the Maryland he loved and for which he worked and prayed so earnestly.

Conditions in Virginia were just as deplorable as in Maryland. In 1671 Governor Berkley reported that, "there are forty-eight parishes, and the ministers well paid. The clergy by my consent would do better if they would pray oftener and preach less. But, as of all commodities, so of this, the worst are sent us."[2] In 1696 the rector of a Virginia parish wrote to the Bishop of London that "several ministers have caused

1. Sweet, op. cit., p. 63.
2. Ibid., p. 55.

such scandals of late" that the people were hesitant to receive a clergyman in many parishes.[3]

The masses of the people sank to lower moral levels in these colonies than did the clergy. It is estimated that not more than one in twenty of the citizens of Virginia was connected with the church in 1700 and that the masses were hostile toward religion.

A similar decadence in religion, with its consequent immorality appeared in the New England colonies. In 1702 Increase Mather published a book entitled, **The Glory Departing from New England.** Mather said:

"We are the posterity of the good old Puritan Non-conformists of England, who were a strict and holy people. Such were our fathers who followed the Lord into the wilderness. O New England, New England, look to it that the glory be not removed from thee, for it begins to go. O, tremble, for it is going; it is gradually departing. You that are aged persons, that can remember what New England was fifty years ago, that saw the Churches in their first glory, is there not a sad decay and diminution of that glory? Time was when these churches were 'beautiful as Tirzah, comely as Jerusalem, terrible as an army with banners.' What a glorious presence of Christ there was in all his ordinances. . . . Many were converted, and there were added to the Churches daily such as should be saved. But are not sound conversions become rare in this day, and in many congregations? Look into the pulpits, and see if there be such a glory there as once there was. When will Boston see a Cotton and a Norton again? When will New England see a Hooker, a Shepherd, a Mitchell, not to mention others?

"Look into the civil state; does Christ reign there as he once did? How many churches, how many towns are there in New England that we may sigh over them, and say, the glory is gone! And there is sad cause to fear that greater departures of the glory are hastening upon us; our iniquities testify against us, and our backslidings are many. That there is a general defection from primitive purity and piety in many

3. *Ibid.*, p. 55.

respects, can not be denied. The providence of God is threatening to pull down the wall which was a defence to the Churches."[4]

This aged and brilliant preacher thus lamented the fact that both Church and State were drifting away from God and righteousness. Similar sentiments were expressed by a younger minister. On May 27, 1730, the Reverend Thomas Prince, junior pastor of the Old South Church of Boston, preached to the General Assembly of the province of Massachusetts. Speaking of the religion and morals of an earlier generation, Prince said:

"And to the great glory of God be it spoken, there never was perhaps before seen such a body of pious people together on the face of earth. Their civil and ecclesiastical leaders were exemplary patterns of piety. They encouraged only the virtuous to come with and follow them. They were so strict, both in the church and the state, that the incorrigible could not endure to live in the country, and went back again. Profane swearers and drunkards were not known in the land. And it quickly grew famous for religion abroad, that scarce any other but those who liked it came over for many years after."[5]

The inference from Prince's statements is that "the incorrigible, the profane swearers and the drunkards" were quite at home in the New England of 1730. The oft quoted words of Jonathan Edwards relative to immorality in Northampton, Massachusetts, may be accepted as an accurate description of immorality in all parts of New England. Edwards said:

"Licentiousness for some years greatly prevailed among the youth of the town; they were many of them addicted to night walking and frequenting the tavern, and lewd practices wherein some of them by their example exceedingly corrupted the others. It was their manner to get together in assemblies of both sexes, for mirth and jollity, which they called frolics;

4. Humphrey, H., *Revival Sketches and Manual*, New York, The American Tract Society, 1939, pp. 65-66.
5. *Ibid.*, p. 67.

and they would often spend the greater part of the night in them, without regard to order in the families they belonged to; indeed family government did too much fail in the town".[6]

Similar conditions prevailed in the middle colonies just prior to the revivals there under the leadership of the Tennents and others. The Reverend Samuel Blair described the situation as follows: "True religion lay, as it were, a dying". He also spoke of, "a lamentable ignorance of the essentials of true practical religion and the doctrines relating thereto".[7]

In all sections of colonial America the light of true religion was all but snuffed out. Immorality was rife in all classes of the population and there was corruption in both church and state. These conditions were brought about, in part, by certain influences which were discussed in the two preceding chapters of this book.

But the appearance of deism in America laid the foundation for this decadent structure of religious and social life. This philosophy denied the revelations of the Old and the New Testaments and taught that the voice of nature was sufficient to guide men in religion and morals. The deists taught that God is, that He created the universe, but that He withdrew from it. He is above His creation, they said, but not in it. He is related to His creation as the dot is to the "i".

Such a conception of God's relationship to the universe makes Him of very little account in the lives of men. Neither His blessings nor His judgment upon human conduct is possible. That He could or would enter into fellowship with men is unthinkable, according to this conception.

This type of philosophical thought spread over the colonies during the last quarter of the seventeenth century. Many prominent Americans held this view when George Whitefield made his evangelistic tours of America just prior to and during the Great Awakening. Decadence in religion and immorality in daily life were the normal fruitage of it.

6. Sweet, *op. cit.*, p. 187.
7. Humphrey, *op. cit.*, p. 68.

CHAPTER IV

THE GREAT AWAKENING IN NEW ENGLAND

The moral and religious conditions in the colonies at the close of the seventeenth century were described in chapter three. This state of affairs continued in New England during the first one-third of the eighteenth century, or until 1734. Such a state of religion and morals cried out to God for a visitation of His power and blessing. The faithful few in all of the churches were in deep distress. Some who had lived through better days complained of "a dry and lifeless state" in the churches.

The first appearance of the dawn of a better day came in the village of Northampton, Massachusetts, in December, 1734. Jonathan Edwards, the brilliant and earnest young pastor of the Congregational Church, was preaching a series of sermons on justification by faith alone when the Spirit of God moved upon the people of the town to inaugurate the revival of religion which history has named, "The Great Awakening".

Edwards was influenced to preach such a series of sermons by the appearance of Arminianism upon the intellectual horizon of his day. Like all other Calvinists, he felt that these doctrines were dangerous. They would lead the people away from a sense of dependence upon Christ for salvation and to the belief that men might be saved because of their own merits. The young Congregational minister felt that such a theory of salvation would lead to the Roman Catholic view. The thesis of his messages was that no act, done by an unconverted man, however good in itself, could avail in procuring salvation, but that salvation is a gift of God alone. He was criticized for introducing such controversial themes into the pulpit but he went on faithfully according to the convictions of his own soul.

Edwards was an effective preacher. His giant intellect, his thorough training, his moral earnestness and his "almost

Oriental fertility of imagination" combined to make him a forceful speaker. His vivid word-pictures of the just wrath of God, the sinfulness of sin, the doom of sinners, and man's impotence to save himself were used of the Holy Spirit to convict of sin and to bring men to repentance.

Edwards describes the beginning of the revival as follows:

"Presently upon this a great and earnest concern about the great things of religion and the eternal world became universal in all parts of the town, and among persons of all degrees and all ages; the noise among the dry bones waxed louder and louder; all other talk but about things spiritual and eternal was soon thrown by; and all conversation in all companies, and upon all occasions, was upon these things only, unless so much as was necessary for people carrying on their ordinary secular business. Other discourse than of the things of religion would scarcely be tolerated in any company".[1]

Within a year, more than three hundred of the citizens of Northampton had professed conversion, but the enthusiasm began to wane before the end of the year. This tendency was brought about in part by the fact that most of the people of the village had been evangelized. There were no more "surprising conversions" to attract attention and to testify to the power of God. Furthermore, the morals of the people had greatly improved. These factors tended to dampen the ardor of the revival, but it went on as a constructive force for several years. In 1743 Edwards wrote:

"Even since the great work of God that was wrought here about nine years ago, there has been a great, abiding alteration in the town in many respects. There has been vastly more religion kept up in the town, among all sorts of persons, in religious exercises, and in common conversation, than used to be before. There has remained a more general seriousness and decency in attending the public worship. —I suppose the town has been in no measure so free from vice,—for any long time together, for this sixty years, as it

1. Sweet, op. cit., pp. 188-89.

has this nine years past. There has also been an evident alteration with respect to a charitable spirit to the poor.—And though, after the great work of nine years ago, there has been a very lamentable decay of religious affections, and the engagedness of people's spirit in religion; yet many societies for prayer and social religion were all along kept up, and there were some few instances of awakening and deep concern about the things of another world, even in the most dead time."[2]

Other communities in New England and New Jersey experienced revivals similar to the Northampton awakening. For example, a revival began in Harvard, Massachusetts, in September, 1739. It is described by Reverend John Seccomb (writing in 1744) as follows:

"The first visible alteration among my people for the better, was some time in the month of September, in the year 1739, when several began to grow more thoughtful and serious, and somewhat reformed; more constant and diligent in attending the public worship, more attentive in hearing the word preached, more careful to sanctify the Sabbath &c.

"Not long after this, came four young men to me under considerable awakenings and concern about their spiritual state. In December following, these same persons were taken into Church fellowship, who had been of too loose a life and conversation in times past; which put many upon further thoughtfulness. From this time, the concern began to increase, and there was scarce a sacrament passed (which is with us once in eight weeks) without some additions to the Church, from that on to the present time; though twelve is the greatest number that have been received at once".[3]

Pastor Seccomb is careful to state that this work was "not done violently nor by strangers." The same trend appears here as in Northampton. Thus the movement began, spread over New England, and had begun to wane when George Whitefield made his memorable visit to this section. His ministry of five weeks was blessed of God to give a new

2. Tracy, J., *The Great Awakening*, Boston, Tippan and Bennett, 1842, p. 21.
3. *Ibid.*, pp. 20-21.

impetus to the work of grace that had been going on for six years.

George Whitefield came to New England from his Orphan House in Savannah, Georgia, at the invitation of many influential clergymen and not a few prominent laymen. His fame as a preacher had preceded him, and many people felt that a revival would begin when he arrived. The awakening, somewhat diminished in enthusiasm, was continuing in many communities, but Tracy says:

"There is even reason to suspect, that the manifestation of revival, which was already secretly at work in men's hearts, was kept back for several months, by the general feeling, that it would take place when Whitefield came, and not before."[4]

An incident which occurred on Sept. 14, 1740—the day following Whitefield's arrival at Newport, Rhode Island—reveals the attitude of many clergymen toward his coming. He received the following letter:

"Reverend Sir and beloved Brother,

"Although mine eyes never saw your face before this day, yet my heart and soul have been united to you in love by the bond of the Spirit. I have longed and expected to see you for many months past. Blessed be God, mine eyes have seen the joyful day. I trust, through grace, I have some things to communicate to you, that will make your heart glad. I shall omit writing anything, and only hereby present my hearty love, and let you know that I am waiting now at the post of your door for admission. Though I am unworthy, my Lord is worthy, in whose name I trust I come. I am your unworthy brother.   Jonathan Barber."[5]

Whitefield had heard of this young man as, "one of those young ministers whom God had lately made use of in such a remarkable manner at the east end of Long Island". He sent for Barber and heard the following story from him:

"He told me that he came to Rhode Island under a full conviction that he should see me there, and had been waiting

4. *Ibid.,* p. 85-86.
5. *Ibid.,* p. 85.

for me eight days; for, he said, these words were mightily impressed upon his heart: 'Is not Aaron the Levite thy brother? I know that he can speak well, and also he cometh forth to meet thee, and when he seeth thee he will be glad in his heart; and I will be with thy mouth, and with his mouth, and will teach you what ye shall do'."[6]

That the people heard Whitefield gladly is revealed by the fact that the legislature adjourned to attend the meetings in Newport. On Thursday the Court at Bristol requested him to preach at noon. As he approached Boston at eight o'clock Thursday evening, he was met by the governor's son, two clergymen, and a number of other citizens. They apologized because the reception committee was so small, explaining that it would have been larger but for a funeral in the town and because of some uncertainty as to when he would arrive. Governor Belcher received him with courtesy and sought many interviews with him.

On Friday afternoon he preached to about four thousand people. The next day six thousand came to hear him in another part of the city. Following this meeting he addressed eight thousand people "on the Common". On Sunday afternoon he preached "to a very thronged auditory, and with great visible effect" in another Boston church.

Thus the great evangelist continued for five weeks, preaching in the larger towns of Rhode Island, Massachusetts, Maine, New Hampshire, and Connecticut. After the public meetings, many people would follow him to his lodging for further prayer and counsel. On October twelfth he preached his farewell sermon on the Boston Common to a crowd estimated at thirty thousand.

In the course of this preaching tour, Whitefield raised the question as to whether or not the ministers had been converted. This caused resentment on the part of some of the clergy, but more than twenty ministers professed conversion under the spell of his preaching. The Reverend John Porter, pastor at Bridgewater, gives the following testimony. Referring to Whitefield he says:

6. *Ibid.*, p. 85.

"Whose name I shall always mention with respect and honor, whatever others may think or say of him, from the benefit one of the meanest and most unworthy of Christ's ministers hopes he received by his holy and fervent ministrations while at Boston. Be sure I knew nothing rightly of my sin and danger, of my need of a Saviour, of the way of salvation by him, neither was established in the doctrines of grace, till I heard that man of God."[7]

Thus the preaching of Whitefield was blessed of God to broaden and deepen the spiritual tides which had begun to ebb in New England. He appeared like a meteor, burned for five weeks, and then returned to Georgia and subsequently to England. The Holy Spirit used him in a mighty way to give new impetus to "The Great Awakening".

Soon after Whitefield's departure, the Reverend Gilbert Tennent came to Boston to continue the work. Whitefield seems to have suggested that he be invited. Tennent, a Presbyterian minister of Pennsylvania, had won fame as an evangelist in revivals which had been going on for some time there and in New Jersey. He arrived in Boston on December thirteenth, 1740, and began an itinerant ministry similar to that of Whitefield. He travelled from church to church and from community to community, preaching three or four times daily and receiving enquirers for personal conferences. This ministry continued for about four months in the Boston area and "in more than two score Massachusetts and Connecticut towns".

The Reverend Thomas Prince, junior pastor of the Old South Church, Boston, at the time of Tennent's visit, wrote:

"As to Tennent's preaching: It was frequently both terrible and searching. It was often for matter justly terrible, as he, according to the inspired oracles, exhibited the dreadful holiness, justice, law, threatenings, truth, power, majesty of God; and His anger with rebellious, impenitent, unbelieving and Christless sinners; the awful danger they were every moment in of being struck down to hell, and being damned

7. *Ibid.*, p. 128.

forever; with the amazing miseries of that place of tor-
ment. . . . . It was not merely, nor so much, his laying open
the terrors of the law and wrath of God, or damnation in hell;
as the laying open their many vain and secret shifts and
refuges, counterfeit resemblances of grace, delusive and
damning hopes, their utter impotence, and impending danger
of destruction; whereby they found all their hopes and refuges
of lies to fail them, and themselves exposed to eternal ruin,
unable to help themselves, and in a lost condition. This
searching preaching was both the suitable and principal
means of their conviction."[8]

One of Tennent's biographers says that, "The influence
of his preaching upon the masses was even greater than that
of Whitefield."[9] On March second, 1741, he preached his farewell sermon in Boston "to an auditory extremely crowded,
very attentive and much affected". Then he returned to
Pennsylvania.

The revival continued unabated for about two years after
Tennent's departure. One Boston preacher said that more
people had sought personal interviews with him, relative to
their spiritual needs, in one week than had come to him in
all the twenty-four years of his ministry before Tennent's
visit. Another testified that six hundred people had sought
personal spiritual guidance in a period of three months, and
still another could count one thousand in the same period.

Persons of all ages and conditions presented themselves to
the pastors for personal help. Prince says:

"There repaired to us both boys and girls, young men
and women, Indians and Negroes, heads of families, aged
persons; those who had been in full communion and going
on in a course of religion many years. . . . Some came under
great temptations; some in great concern for their souls;
some in great distress of mind for fear of being unconverted;
others for fear they had been all along building on a righteous-

8. *Ibid.*, p. 116.
9. Sweet, W. W., *Makers of American Christianity*, New York, Henry
   Holt and Co., 1937, p. 91.

ness of their own, and were still in the gall of bitterness and the bond of iniquity."[10]

This interest on the part of the people demanded more preaching. The regular services on Sunday and the lecture on Thursday evening did not satisfy. The number of week-day lectures was increased to five per week in many Boston churches. Private societies were formed to meet in the homes of the people to which the ministers were invited. One pastor said, "The more we prayed and preached, the more enlarged were our hearts, and the more delightful the employment. And, O how many, how serious and attentive the hearers! How many awakened and hopefully converted by their ministers!"[11]

This work of grace was not confined to the Boston area. It appeared at Wrentham in a revival which was not promoted "by traveling ministers" but by the pastors of the two churches in the community. One pastor said that, "Our people grew very desirous of lectures, that they might have more frequent opportunity for spiritual instruction, and to join in social worship, where we found God often bestowed His blessing."[12] At Bridgewater the revival fires were rekindled by the testimonies of two young men who had been influenced by the awakening in Connecticut. These men, natives of Bridgewater, secured permission to conduct a service for the young people. But, when the time came for the meeting, people of all ages were in attendance. After a period of worship, the young men gave, "a friendly Christian exhortation". The blessing of God was so evident upon this first meeting that the youthful exhorters continued with similar meetings for several weeks. There were many awakenings and conversions through their efforts.

The eagerness of the people to hear the gospel and the success of the itinerant ministries of Whitefield and Tennent were used of the Holy Spirit to bring several men into the

10. Tracy, op. cit., p. 117.
11. Ibid., p. 119.
12. Ibid., p. 123.

work as travelling evangelists. Many pastors gave part of their time to meetings in communities outside their regular parishes. Jonathan Edwards was often invited to preach and conduct evangelistic meetings in many parts of New England. It was during one of these meetings that he preached his famous sermon on "Sinners in the Hands of an Angry God" from the text, "Their foot shall slide in due time" (Deut. 32:35). Before he had finished his sermon, "The assembly appeared deeply impressed and bowed down with an awful conviction of their sin and danger. There was such a breathing of distress and weeping, that the preacher was obliged to speak to the people and desire silence, that he might be heard."[13] A contemporary describes Edwards' work as a travelling evangelist in these words: "Whithersoever he turned himself, he seems to have prospered."[14] Other pastors, in all parts of New England, began to give part of their time to evangelistic meetings beyond the borders of their own local fields of labor.

Then there were some ministers who gave all of their time to itinerant evangelism. Eleazer Wheelock was not a settled pastor but he was received enthusiastically by most of the ministers and was welcomed to preach in their pulpits. His private journal reveals that he travelled from place to place, preaching three or four times daily. His sermon produced deep conviction of sin and resulted in many conversions. Like Whitefield and Tennent, Wheelock spent much time in personal interviews with interested inquirers.

The people were anxious to hear the Word of God as it was preached by Wheelock. Of his ministry in Bridgewater, Massachusetts, he made the following entry in his private journal:

"Nov. 9—Visited this morning with a great number of persons under soul trouble. Refused to preach because I designed to go out of town. Just as I was going, came Mr. Webb and told me that the people were meeting together to hear an-

13. *Ibid.*, p. 216.
14. *Ibid.*, p. 217.

other sermon. I consented to preach again. A scholar from Cambridge being present, who came to get me to go to Cambridge, hastened to Cambridge, and by a little after six, a great part of the scholars had got to Boston. Preached to a thronged assembly, many more than could get into the house, with very great freedom and enlargement."[15]

In all parts of New England pastors, pastor-evangelists, and itinerant evangelists preached to eager throngs for some two years after Tennent's departure. Many were converted and added to the churches. From 1740 to 1742 there were fifty thousand additions to the churches of New England out of a total population of some three hundred thousand. Many pastors gave testimony that the people of the churches showed evidence of growth in character as a result of the Great Awakening.

But certain influences began to operate against the revival by the end of 1742. The emotional excesses which began to appear were attacked by the Rev. Charles Chauncy, pastor of the First Church Boston. In 1743 he published a pamphlet entitled, "Seasonable Thoughts on the State of Religion in New England," to which Jonathan Edwards made reply. Ministers flocked to the support of both men and there was much acrimonious debate on the merits and demerits of the revival.

These emotional excesses appeared in all parts of New England. Mention has already been made of the outcries while Edwards was preaching in Enfield on "Sinners in the Hands of an Angry God". There were faintings and convulsions in this same meeting. The Rev. Eleazer Wheelock made the following entry into his private journal on Nov. 1, 1741: "Went with brother Bryan to Taunton; preached there, one cried out. Appointed another meeting in the evening. I believe thirty cried out. . . . I was forced to break off my sermon before it was done, the outcry was so great."[16] These demonstrations were likely caused, in part, by the physical exhaustion from so many meetings and so much fear.

14. *Ibid.*, p. 203.
16. *Ibid.*, p. 202.

But the minister whose work produced the most extreme phenomena was the Rev. James Davenport of Long Island. Davenport came to Connecticut "on or about July 14, 1741". He had been with Whitefield and was commended by him. Under his preaching, there were "trances and visions". He asserted that the ministers were unconverted, saying that they "were blind guides, leading the people blind-folded into hell."[17] On May 29, 1742, a complaint was filed against him in court and he was arrested. In the course of the trial, when the sheriff was escorting him to his lodging, he attempted to speak to the crowd that followed. When he was denied the privilege, the mob attacked the sheriff's party. The court pronounced him insane and deported him.

These conditions divided the ministers. Those who favored the revival and defended its methods were called "New Lights". Jonathan Edwards became the leader of this group. Those who criticised the excesses and opposed the revival were named "Old Lights". Their leader was Rev. Charles Chauncy. In the churches too some of the members followed the "New Lights" and others supported the "Old Lights." These divisions caused a sad decline in evangelistic fervor.

The outbreak of "King George's War" in 1744 sounded the death knell of the Great Awakening in New England. The war lasted four years. Both New England and the Middle Colonies were involved. Money, soldiers, and supplies were furnished by Pennsylvania, New Jersey, New York, Connecticut, and Rhode Island, but Massachusetts bore the brunt of it. War and evangelism do not prosper together. This intercolonial war marked the final decline of that revival of religion which deserves to be called, "The Great Awakening."

Some new methods in evangelism appeared during this ten years of spiritual renewal. Itinerant evangelists did not appear upon the New England scene until the arrival of George Whitefield, but after his visit this type of worker became frequent. Open-air preaching was introduced by Whitefield because the crowds that came to hear him were too large to

17. *Ibid.*, p. 236.

be accommodated in church buildings. Personal counsel and prayer came to be practiced because so many people sought personal help. Also "private societies" were organized for worship, Bible study and evangelism. In these "cottage prayer meetings" the pastors preached, prayed, and exhorted with good results. Lay exhorters also appeared but lost most of their influence because of their association with the unfortunate Davenport. Most of these methods have persisted in various parts of the United States since the Great Awakening.

CHAPTER V

SPIRITUAL RENEWAL IN THE MIDDLE COLONIES

Religious awakenings, similar to the Great Awakening of New England, began in the colonies of New Jersey, Pennsylvania, and New York some fourteen years before the Northampton revival. The foundation for such a movement had been laid by the settling of certain religious groups in this area who had been influenced by Pietism. This great evangelistic movement began, however, in 1720 when the Reverend Theodore Frelinghuysen came to be pastor of four Dutch Reformed Churches in the Raritan Valley in New Jersey.

Frelinghuysen was a German Pietist, a product of the University of Halle, Germany, which was the center of the Pietistic movement. This zealous minister began his career in the colony by attacking the dead formalism which pervaded the Dutch Reformed Churches in the colonies. He, like all Pietists, preached the necessity of a vital religious experience and a genuine moral reformation. Such evangelical doctrines aroused opposition from the very beginning. Within three years, the four churches of which Frelinghuysen was pastor were divided and the Dutch ministers were arrayed in two hostile factions. The opposition of certain ministers hastened the disruption of his churches. Boel, junior pastor of the Dutch Reformed Church in New York, even visited Frelinghuysen's congregations and organized them to oppose their pastor and the evangelistic movement which was in the making.

But opposition and divisions did not dampen the ardor of this evangelist, neither did they seem to hinder the movement very much. Many young people were converted through the ministry of Frelinghuysen and even the elders and deacons of his four churches professed conversion one after another.

The last deacon made his new confession in 1725.[1] Such results awakened the interest of the faithful in other communities and the pastor began an itinerant evangelistic ministry. His preaching was blessed of God to produce awakenings and conversions in other communities, but his method became the object of criticism. A New York lawyer said in scorn, "Why does he not stay with those congregations whose minister he is and first seek out the many unconverted souls that are there, instead of depriving them of spiritual food by going so often to other places?"[2]

Many pamphlets were circulated against him charging him with heresy, but the revival spread throughout the Raritan Valley, and in 1726 it was destined to touch the Presbyterian Church and to spread over all of the Middle Colonies.

Two innovations, besides itinerant preaching, were introduced by Frelinghuysen during the early years of the movement. He led in the formation of small groups who met for prayer and Bible study. He had known such group meetings among the Pietists of Germany. The conservatives attacked this practice because the meetings were held in the homes of the people. Such "secret meetings" must be of questionable character, they said. Frelinghuysen's second departure from the path of tradition was the introduction of "lay preachers", whom he called helpers. Both of these new methods were severely criticised by the opposition party.

In 1726 Frelinghuysen met young Gilbert Tennent who was to become the foremost preacher among the Presbyterians supporting the revival. Tennent's first pastorate was a small Presbyterian Church in the Raritan Valley. Frelinghuysen welcomed the young minister and urged the members of the Dutch Reformed congregations to help in his financial support. The two pastors became intimate friends, often holding joint services. Frelinghuysen would preach in Dutch and Tennent in English at such meetings. His fellowship with Ten-

1. Maxson, C. H., *The Great Awakening*, Chicago, University of Chicago Press, 1920, p. 16.
2. *Ibid.*, p. 26.

nent brought a fresh storm of criticism upon the pastor of the Dutch churches. The use of the English language was "irregular" and the joint observance of the Lord's Supper was termed "a sacrilege".[3] Thus the revival grew to interdenominational proportions by 1726 and the opposition grew in extent and bitterness.

The appearance of Gilbert Tennent introduced the famous Tennent family and another stream of spiritual life which contributed much to the Great Awakening in the Middle Colonies. The Reverend William Tennent came to America from Ireland in 1718. After preaching "with wondrous zeal" in several communities, he became pastor at Neshaminy, Pennsylvania, in 1726. Here he built a log house in which he trained his four sons and other young men for the ministry. From this "Log College," as it was called in derision, several ministers went forth to be a blessing to the world during the Great Awakening in this section of colonial America and beyond the borders of the Middle Colonies.

The meeting of these two streams of spiritual life—the one originating in Germany and the other in Ireland—produced a river of vital spiritual religion which was destined to sweep over all of colonial America.

Gilbert Tennent, the oldest son of William Tennent, played the leading role among the Presbyterians in the Middle Colonies. He also preached with great success in New England. He was influenced by his distinguished father who trained him at his Log College and also by Frelinghuysen. During a period of illness in 1726, young Tennent was depressed by the fruitlessness of his ministry. As he compared the results of his preaching with the accomplishments of Frelinghuysen, he resolved to adopt the direct and searching methods of his new friend. This decision marked the beginning of his unusual effectiveness as an evangelist.[4] Thus the two "rivers of living water" mentioned above were united in one life.

The other sons of William Tennent preached with suc-

3. *Ibid.*, p. 17.
4. *Ibid.*, p. 31.

cess during this period of spiritual renewal. John Tennent became pastor of the Presbyterian Church at Freehold, New Jersey, in 1729. He was a retiring, compassionate mystic, but his preaching won many to Christ during his brief ministry. He died in 1732, and was succeeded in the Freehold pastorate by his youngest brother, William Tennent, Jr. This youngest of the Tennent brothers enjoyed a long and useful ministry in New Jersey.

Several Log College graduates besides the Tennents were used of God to promote the revival. John Cross, pastor at Basking Ridge, led in a revival in 1734-1735 which resulted in three hundred conversions. This success at home brought many invitations for meetings and Cross enjoyed an extensive itinerant ministry. Samuel Blair, John Rowland, and Aaron Burr, Sr., were also ardent and effective supporters of the revival.

Opposition to the awakening appeared early among the Presbyterians. It led to a division into two groups—"The Old Side," opposing Log College men, and the "New Side", which was led by them. A new Presbytery, known as the New Brunswick Presbytery, was organized by the "New Side" group in 1738. This division affected practically every Presbyterian congregation in the Middle Colonies. The "Great Schism" which came in this manner was finally healed in 1758. Gilbert Tennent was influential in bringing about a reconciliation.

This spiritual awakening had appeared among the Dutch Reformed and the Presbyterians and had encountered strong opposition by 1739. It had grown so steadily in spite of opposition that the tides were strong and deep when George Whitefield appeared on the scene on October thirtieth, 1739.

Whitefield landed at Lewes, Delaware, on October thirtieth and was in Philadelphia on November second. He made the journey on horseback. The newspapers in the colony had published stories telling of the phenomenal success of this young preacher in England and arousing much interest. Because the church buildings of Philadelphia were too small to seat the crowds that flocked to hear him, Whitefield preached in the open air as he had been doing in England. The second story balcony of the court house in Philadelphia became his pulpit. From this elevated platform he preached to vast throngs in the street below. He also preached daily on "Society Hill" to large crowds. Tracy says that, "great numbers were awakened, not only in the various denominations of professed Christians, but among those who had wholly neglected religion."[5]

From Philadelphia, Whitefield traveled to New York. It was a journey of conquest. He preached to large crowds along the way with the following results: "Ministers and people shedding tears; sinners struck with awe; and serious persons, who had been much run down and despised, filled with joy."[6]

The Church of England was closed to Whitefield in New York, but he was invited to preach in the Presbyterian Church. This building was too small to accommodate the crowds, however. This led to his preaching in the fields as he had done in England before coming to America. Many were awakened and converted through this ministry.

While in Philadelphia, Whitefield met William Tennent, Jr. On the journey from Philadelphia to New York, he was introduced to William Tennent, Sr., and his eldest son, Gilbert Tennent. Other young men who had been trained in the elder Tennent's Log College also came under the influence of Whitefield during this period. The evangelistic zeal of the Tennents and their associates found a ready response in Whitefield and he cast his lot with them in the evangelistic movement. Here another stream of spiritual life which found its source in the Pietistic movement in Germany and its course in the Wesleyan revival of England, came to add its power to the spiritual tides which were sweeping over the colonies of America. The Spirit of God had moved upon the life of Germany, which centered in the University of Halle. Both Wesley and Whitefield were influenced by the Pietists. Freling-

5. Tracy, *op. cit.*, p.
6. *Ibid.*, p. 53.

huysen had come directly from Germany and the fellowship of German Pietists to be the leader of the revival movement among the Dutch Reformed Churches. He had also influenced young Gilbert Tennent, but the elder Tennent had come from Ireland and was a flaming evangelist before he had fellowship with Frelinghuysen or Whitefield. Thus German Pietism and Irish Presbyterianism had been used of the Holy Spirit to start the movement. The coming of Whitefield brought the movement to high tide in 1740.

Whitefield finished his first tour of the Middle Colonies in December, 1739, but the revival went on with unabated zeal after his departure. A notable awakening occurred in Newark, New Jersey, under the preaching of Aaron Burr and John Dickinson. Some emotional excesses appeared here but the leaders sought to repress them. Another revival came to the highlands of New York through the ministry of William Tennent, Jr., and other Log College graduates. The center of the movement in Pennsylvania seems to have been at Fagg's Manor, where Samuel Blair preached with unusual power. Blair also sought to discourage the emotional excesses which appeared here. Interested people from other communities visited the revival at Fagg's Manor and returned to their own communities with new zeal. The movement was spreading over all of the Middle Colonies when Whitefield returned for his second tour of this area.

Whitefield arrived at New Castle, Delaware, to begin this second evangelistic journey on April thirteenth, 1740. This itinerary was much like the first. He retraced his steps and preached to equally large and enthusiastic crowds. Many were converted and a marked moral reformation ensued. One new feature appeared, however, at this time. The evangelist collected money for his Orphan House at Savannah, Georgia, and planned schools for the Negroes. He denounced the abuse of slaves but did not attack the institution of slavery. Philanthropy and Christian education thus found their inspiration and support in the Great Awakening.

It was during this second visit of Whitefield that the movement began to bear fruit in other Christian groups besides the Presbyterians and the Dutch Reformed. While in Philadelphia, Whitefield heard a sermon by the Reverend Jenkins Jones, pastor of the Baptist Church. He was impressed by his preaching. Whitefield said, "He is the only preacher I know of in Philadelphia who speaks feelingly and with authority." It was in Pennsylvania, also, that the great evangelist had fellowship with the Moravians for the first time. Peter Boehler, a Moravian missionary, traveled with Whitefield through the Moravian settlements, serving as his interpreter. This group was thoroughly evangelical and somewhat evangelistic before the coming of Whitefield, but they were inspired and strengthened by him. They became influential in the revival movement. The Quakers of this area, who had played such an important role in the evangelism of the previous century, were refreshed and renewed by the ministry of Whitefield at this time.

This broadening of the scope of the revival aroused the critics. The attacks of the preachers in the revival upon the opposing clergy had been resented from the very beginning. About this time, however, Gilbert Tennent preached a sermon at Nottingham on "The Dangers of an Unconverted Ministry" which added fresh fuel to the smouldering fires of resentment. The opposing clergy seized the opportunity presented by some emotional excesses to attack the movement openly. From this time forward the opposition was outspoken and aggressive. After Whitefield's departure there was much itinerant preaching by Gilbert Tennent, Jonathan Dickinson, and other evangelists. The results were gratifying but the emotional excesses which had been attacked by the opposition appeared more and more. The revival was proceeding with great power and the opposition was increasing in intensity when Whitefield returned for a third itinerary of these colonies.

The third tour of the Middle Colonies began during the last days of October, 1740. His schedule included most of the communities he had visited on the two previous campaigns. The crowds and the response were just as remarkable as they had been before, but the opposition was more aggressive and outspoken. It was during this period that the "Old Side" Presbyterians who resented his alliance with the Tennents, published a tract in which they attacked Whitefield as, "A Papist under disguise as a Calvinist."[7] They replied to the insinuations that the ministers were unconverted by questioning the genuineness of the conversions during the revival period. They asserted that, since these new converts had shown no interest in religion before, the reality of their experiences might well be called in question. Whitefield and his associates made reply to these charges and a serious controversy ensued.

After 1740 the spiritual tides subsided somewhat, but the movement went on winning many to Christ until the American Revolution involved all of the colonies. Several philanthropic, educational, and missionary agencies came into being during this period as a result of the revival. They will be discussed in a later chapter.

7. Maxson, *op. cit.*, p. 66.

CHAPTER VI

REVIVAL FIRES IN THE SOUTH

Revival fires were started in the South when the Reverend William Robinson visited Virginia in 1742. Robinson, a Log College graduate, was sent out by the New Brunswick Presbytery of New Jersey to visit the scattered groups of Presbyterians of Virginia and North Carolina. The brief tour of this flaming evangelist resulted in the organization of several Presbyterian congregations composed of immigrants from New Jersey and Pennsylvania and new converts who had been won by Robinson. The immigrants had been influenced by the Great Awakening in the Middle Colonies.

When Robinson had completed his itinerary, he was invited to preach at Hanover, Virginia, where the Church of England was the only active church. A strange revival had begun here without a preacher. A small group of earnest people had been driven to near-despair by the decadent condition of the church and the low moral standards of the clergy. It is said that even the reading of the prayers by these men was so insincere as to be a matter of levity. This condition cried out to God for a visitation of His power and blessing and this small group had found the fellowship of the Holy Spirit even before Robinson came.

The first leader of this movement was Samuel Morris. He invited a few friends to visit his home at regular intervals to read Luther's Commentary on Galatians, a book of George Whitefield's sermons, and similar literature. The crowds grew to such proportions that it became necessary to erect a house of worship to accommodate them. It was called "Morris's Reading House". Morris said: "My dwelling house was at length too small to contain the people, whereupon we determined to build a meeting house for reading."[1] The re-

1. Geweher, W. M., *The Great Awakening in Virginia*, Durham, N. C., Duke University Press, 1930, p. 48.

sults at Hanover were so remarkable that Morris was pressed into an extensive itinerant ministry. The meetings he conducted offered no other form of worship or instruction than the public reading of religious books.

This state of religion and morals in Hanover presents a true picture of the situation in general. Immorality was rife among all classes. The wealthy planters along the eastern seaboard were addicted to gambling and drinking. Horse racing and cock fighting were the principal sports. On the western side of the Blue Ridge Mountains, pioneer conditions prevailed with typical immorality. There were no schools or churches in many communities and drunkenness prevailed among many.

Three conditions—decadence in the Established Church, immorality among all classes of people, and spiritual hunger on the part of the few—gave Robinson a favorable hearing everywhere, especially at Hanover. He preached there for four days to large crowds. Morris, writing in 1750, says:

"Such of us as had been hungering for the word before, were lost in agreeable surprise and astonishment, and some could not refrain from publicly declaring their transports. . . . Many that came through curiosity were pricked to the heart, and but few in the numerous assemblies on those four days appeared unaffected. They returned alarmed with apprehensions of their dangerous condition, convinced of their former ignorance of religion and anxiously inquiring what they should do to be saved."[2]

Because the Reading House was too small to accommodate the crowds, these meetings were held in the open.

The scattered groups who had been won by Morris and other "Readers" became Presbyterians under the influence of Robinson. At his suggestion, they added public prayer and the singing of the Psalms to their worship.

The revival in Virginia and North Carolina was promoted by traveling evangelists from 1743 to 1748. These men were

2. *Ibid.,* p. 51

Log College graduates and were revivalists of the extreme type. They attacked the Church of England, especially the delinquency of the clergy, with such vigor that out-spoken opposition to the revival was aroused. This opposition, which had hailed some of the "Reading House" group into court previously, caused the arrest and trial of several of the itinerant evangelists. It also aroused a doctrinal controversy which was most acrimonious. This condition tended to decrease the zeal of the revivalists by 1748. At this date the Reverend Samuel Davis came to be pastor of the Presbyterian group in Hanover. This brilliant preacher remained for many years and was useful in directing the spiritual energies which had been released by the revival into constructive work. The evangelistic movement continued among the Presbyterians, but with less zeal and effectiveness, until the outbreak of the Revolutionary War.

In 1754 the Reverend Shubal Stearns, a Baptist minister from Connecticut, settled in Virginia where he was joined a little later by Daniel Marshall, his brother-in-law. Both of these men had been converted in the Great Awakening in New England.[3] They were known as Separate Baptists because they had broken with the Regular Baptists of New England because of the revival there. The Regular Baptists were not aggressively evangelistic up to this time. Their part in the Great Awakening in New England and in the Middle Colonies had been negligible. They had received many influential members in New England, however, because of the agitation there about church polity and other doctrines.

The removal of Stearns and Marshall to Virginia marked the beginning of Baptist activity and influence in the period of revival which began with the Northampton revival in New England and had spread over the Middle Colonies and into the Southern Colonies. These evangelists preached in Virginia for a few months but were hindered by opposition of the Baptists in the Old Dominion. In 1755 they removed to Sandy Creek in Guilford County, North Carolina. Here they organ-

3. Sweet, W. W., *The Story of Religions in America*, New York, Harper and Bros., 1930, pp. 219-221.

ized the Sandy Creek Baptist Church, which was destined to be the center of a farreaching evangelistic movement. Stearns was the first pastor of this church.

The Sandy Creek Church was organized with sixteen members. In a very short time the membership had grown to six hundred and six. Five years later the Sandy Creek Baptist Association was organized. This has been called the "Mother Association," and the Sandy Creek Church has the reputation of being, "the mother, grandmother and great-grandmother of forty-two churches."[4]

From this center Baptist evangelists traveled in every direction, preaching with great power, winning thousands to Christ, and organizing churches. Their work covered much of Maryland, Carolina, Tennessee, Kentucky and Pennsylvania. In spite of strong and bitter opposition in Virginia, there were fifty-four Baptist Churches with four thousand and four members in that colony alone by 1774. The growth in the other colonies mentioned was quite as remarkable as it was in Virginia.

These accomplishments were the results, almost entirely, of the preaching of these itinerant evangelists. Samuel Harris preached in Culpeper and Orange Counties in Virginia. It is said that people sometimes traveled a hundred miles to hear him preach and that it was common for people to come to his meetings from a distance of forty or fifty miles. Many would camp at the place of meeting in order to attend the services for several consecutive days.

The following description of the ministry of Harris and one of his co-laborers has been preserved:

"In one of their visits, they baptized seventy-five persons at one time, and in the course of one of their journeys, which usually lasted for several weeks, they baptized upwards of two hundred. It was not uncommon at one of their great meetings for many hundreds to camp on the grounds, in order to be present next day."[5]

4. *Ibid.,* p. 220.
5. *Ibid.,* p. 220.

Here is the first appearance of the "Camp Meeting" which became so popular in a later period of American history.

Emotional excesses and bodily exercises appeared in these meetings. They were not discouraged by the ministers who believed that they were evidences of the work of the Holy Spirit in convicting of sin. Such bodily exercises as "jerks," trembling, falling on the ground, crying and even "barking" like dogs were not uncommon. These phenomena, however, do not seem to have hindered the awakening here as did the emotional excesses in the Great Awakening in New England.

The Baptists suffered severe persecution everywhere. They traveled at their own expense, sought no remuneration from the people they served, and gave themselves without stint, but the people to whom they preached the gospel subjected them to terrible indignities. In 1771 John Waller was severely beaten. The Anglican clergyman, his secretary and the sheriff led in the attack. The clergyman ran his whip down Waller's throat to silence him and he was then given a severe beating. When his persecutors had left, however, Waller continued the sermon which they had interrupted. Others of these itinerant evangelists were kicked, dragged by the hair, and submerged in mud until they were nearly drowned. On one occasion at least, a live snake and a hornet's nest were used in breaking up a meeting.[6]

The persecution which these noble men of God endured was not given the sanction of law until 1768. After that date their persecution was legal in Virginia, where the Church of England was the State Church. Many were imprisoned for preaching without legal permits. Others were fined for not attending the Anglican Church as the law required of all citizens. The ministers bore this legal persecution because they believed that the State had no right to decide whether a man could preach or not. They believed that they were called of God and that any intervention by a human government was a sacrilege.

The sentiment for freedom in Virginia was perhaps the

6. Gewehr, op. cit., p. 120.

cause for a change in policy. The Baptists were no longer imprisoned for preaching without the permission of the State nor were they fined for not attending the worship of the Established Church. The preachers were arrested as disturbers of the peace. Often their enemies would seek to destroy them while they were in prison. The enemies of James Ireland tried to blow up the jail of Culpeper County, Virginia, in 1770 because that evangelist was imprisoned there as a disturber of the peace.

Scores of Baptist ministers were subjected to mob violence and imprisoned by process of law, but their influence grew steadily. The patience with which they suffered injustice, their loyalty to their convictions, and their Christ-like attitude toward their tormenters were powerful in moving men toward God.

Two other factors contributed to the phenomenal success of this group of preachers whom Gewehr calls "the revivers of the revival." In the first place, they were of the common people. They spoke their language and lived on their plane socially and economically. The plain people had not been reached by the awakening in these colonies until the coming of Stearns and Marshall. These men with their associates brought the gospel to the poorest of the poor with transparent sincerity and flaming zeal. It may be said of them, as it was said of their Lord, that, "the common people heard them gladly."

As the period of the American Revolution approached, the political leaders of Virginia and the other colonies found that their ideas of political freedom and democracy were akin to the ideas of these Baptists concerning religious freedom and church polity. This gave the Baptists an influence among leaders of life and thought which they did not possess before. The course of events which brought about the Revolution and the independence of the thirteen colonies made it possible for the Baptists to grow in influence as well as in numbers.

The Separate Baptists continued their effective and far-reaching evangelism up to the outbreak of the American Revo-

lution. By 1770, the Sandy Creek Association had grown so
that it was necessary to divide it. Three associations were
formed, one in North Carolina, one in South Carolina and another in Virginia. At the meeting of the Virginia association
in 1771, the churches reported a membership of 1,335, but the
membership had grown to 3,195 two years later.[7]

The near approach of the war and some doctrinal disputes began to retard the evangelistic work of the Baptists
by 1775. The terrific struggle for religious liberty and the
separation of the Church and State after the war absorbed
the attention of the Baptists and continued to retard their
work of evangelism. But this declension was for a few years
only. The Baptists were to play an important role in evangelism from this period to the present time.

The revival in Virginia received new emphasis from 1773
to the close of the Revolution through the ministry of the
Reverend Devereux Jarrett, an Anglican clergyman, and
the Methodists. Jarrett had been converted through the influence of the New Side Presbyterians, but he accepted orders
in the Anglican Church because he felt that this church would
afford him a larger field of influence. He also believed the
episcopal form of church government to be of divine origin.

Jarrett was almost alone in the Church of England in
his evangelistic zeal. All of the clergy frowned upon him and
his work except the Reverend Archibald McRoberts. This
fact indicates the decadent condition of that Church. Jarrett
says, in his autobiography: "I was opposed and reproached by
the clergy, called an enthusiast, fanatic, visionary, dissenter,
Presbyterian madman, and what not."[8] This attitude on the
part of the State Church of Virginia prepared the way for the
evangelistic preaching of the other groups.

The pulpit messages of Jarrett were very similar to the
preaching of Jonathan Edwards and Gilbert Tennent. He
said: "I endeavored to expose, in the most alarming colors,

7. Newman, A. H., *A History of the Baptist Churches in the United
States*, New York, The Christian Literature Co., 1894, pp. 300 ff.
8. Gewehr, *op. cit.*, p. 138.

the guilt of sin, the entire depravity of human nature—the awful danger mankind are in by nature and practice—the tremendous curse to which they are obnoxious, and their utter inability to evade the sentence of the law and the strokes of divine justice by their own power, merit or good works."[9] He also emphasized the pietistic teaching of a vital personal religious experience and a thorough reformation of morals.

Two new methods in evangelism were introduced by Jarrett—prayer meetings in private homes and the testimony meeting. This procedure was probably suggested by the experience of Frelinghuysen in New Jersey some years before. The personal testimony phase seems to have developed spontaneously in the meetings of small groups for prayer and Bible study.

The success of Jarrett's ministry in his own parish in the county of Bath attracted attention in the other parishes near by. People came from other sections to hear him preach and returned with a zeal for evangelism. The crowds that waited upon his pulpit ministry grew to such proportions that Jarrett had to preach in the fields. The meeting houses were too small to accommodate the people who came from far and near. Invitations began to come for the pastor to preach in other communities and he began an itinerant ministry which took him into several counties. By 1773 his field of labor "had extended to a circle of five or six hundred miles—east, west, north and south."[10]

The work of this zealous minister was doomed to failure in the Anglican Church. It found an outlet, however, in the Methodist Church which was, at that date, a part of the Church of England. Robert Williams, a lay preacher in the Wesleyan revival in England, came to Virginia in 1772. Jarrett describes him as a "plain, simple-hearted, pious man . . . an artless, indefatigable preacher of the gospel." He and Mr. Jarrett were soon fast friends and co-laborers, a relationship which continued until the death of Williams in 1775.

9. *Ibid.*, p. 139.
10. *Ibid.*, p. 141.

Williams, sent by John Wesley, was the first Methodist preacher to come to America. He preached his first sermon in the colony at Norfolk from the court house steps. After singing a hymn and kneeling for prayer, he preached to a rather boisterous audience but a great revival began in spite of the disrespectful attitude. It spread so rapidly that Williams could report one hundred members within one year. By the close of 1774, their adherents numbered two hundred and eighteen. In this same year the first Methodist circuit in Virginia was formed. Two other preachers, Joseph Pilmoor and William Watters, had come to join Williams and Jarrett in the latter part of 1772.

The Methodist revival, which began as a movement within the Anglican Church, reached high tide in 1775-1776. Williams visited Bishop Asbury in April, 1775, to report the work in the South. Asbury made the following entry in his journal as of April 28, 1775: "I met with Brother Williams from Virginia, who gave me a great account of the work of God in those parts—five or six hundred souls justified by faith, and five or six circuits formed."[11] Thus the revival spread over three colonies in a short period of three years. Crowds were often so large that the meetings had to be held in the fields. In the one year of 1775, six hundred members were added to the New Brunswick circuit under the preaching of George Shadford, lately arrived from England. A total of eighteen hundred members were added to the Methodist Societies in Virginia alone during this same year.

In the Spring of 1776 the revival began to wane. This was caused by the outbreak of war and by some emotional excesses. The fact that the Methodists were still in the Church of England was a great disadvantage to them. Shadford left the New Brunswick circuit and returned to England in 1776 because he was a loyal subject of the crown as well as a clergyman in the Church of England.[12]

The emotional reactions which had appeared in other revivals of this half-century accompanied the Methodist re-

11. *Ibid.*, p. 145.
12. *Ibid.*, pp. 156-157.

vival. They also occurred in Jarrett's meetings but he sought to repress them. But the Methodist ministers were willing for the emotional tides to run high. A local preacher in Sussex wrote to Jarrett on July 29, 1776, that "it is common with us for men and women to fall down as dead under an exhortation; but many more under prayer; perhaps twenty at a time. And some of them have fallen to earth, have shown the same distress, wringing their hands, smiting their breasts, and begging all to pray for them."[13] Another contemporary said:

"I have been at meetings where the whole congregation was bathed in tears; and sometimes their cries would be so loud that the preacher's voice could not be heard. Some would be seized with a trembling, and in a few minutes drop to the floor as if they were dead; while others were embracing each other with streaming eyes, and all were lost in wonder, love and praise."[14]

Certain factors, besides the operations of the Divine Spirit and the power of the gospel, contributed to the phenomenal success of the Methodists during this brief period. They preached the necessity of a vital, personal religious experience. The conversions produced real moral reformation and they found genuine joy in their Christian experiences. Like the Baptists, they ministered to the masses of the people. This gave them a large constituency. Their music was also powerful in winning men to Christ. The hymns of John and Charles Wesley and of others contained gospel truth and made a mighty appeal to the people. Their relationship with the Church of England hindered them during the Revolution and for some years after, but they were destined to a great future in America.

These sweeping revivals in the South drew inspiration from four human sources—the Presbyterian revivals in the Middle Colonies, the spontaneous revival at Hanover, the Great Awakening in New England, and the Wesleyan re-

13. *Ibid.*, p. 152.
14. *Ibid.*, p. 153.

vival in England. It has been noted that John Robinson
came from the New Brunswick Presbytery in Pennsylvania to
visit Presbyterian immigrants in the Southern Colonies.
These immigrants and Robinson brought the zeal of the New
Side Presbyterians into this area. Robinson was influential
in winning Jarrett to Christ. He also found and directed
the spontaneous awakening in Hanover which had produced
the "Reading House revivals" of that section. Shubal Stearns
and Daniel Marshall were converts of the New England awakening. Their coming to Virginia and North Carolina marked
the beginning of the far-reaching evangelism among the Baptists. The first Methodist preachers—Robert Williams,
Joseph Pilmoor, William Watters, and George Shadford
—came from England, having been sent out by John Wesley.
The movement went into eclipse during the Revolution but
the foundation had been laid for an extensive work after
the war and the period of adjustment which followed.

CHAPTER VII

SOME CONTRIBUTIONS OF
COLONIAL EVANGELISM TO AMERICAN LIFE

The period of revivals which is called The Great Awakening closed with the outbreak of the American Revolution. The movement had subsided in New England and in the Middle Colonies a few years prior to that date, but it was sweeping the Southern Colonies when hostilities began. It was continuing in New England and the Middle Colonies as a mighty constructive force, even though conversions were not so numerous as they had been in the earlier years and emotional excesses were less in evidence. The curtain fell upon this mighty awakening all over America, however, during the struggle for independence. The results of this visitation of the Holy Spirit continued in many valuable, permanent contributions to the life of the nation.

There were thousands of conversions in all the colonies in these revivals. Complete statistics are not available but there were fifty thousand conversions in New England alone during the years of 1741 and 1742. One sixth of the people of these colonies were converted in the brief period of two years. Other thousands were won to Christ in other colonies during all of the years of the revival period. The influence of these twice-born men and women was a potent factor in winning others and in establishing Christianity in the New World.[1]

There was a marked moral reformation in all of Colonial America as a result of this revival movement. Jonathan Edwards' familiar description of the change in the village of Northampton may be taken as descriptive of the results in other communities. The teaching that a genuine moral

1. Sweet, *op. cit.*, p. 193.

reformation must result from conversion had been promulgated through the ministries of Frelinghuysen and Whitefield.

The beginnings of benevolent institutions in America appeared in the Great Awakening era. Whitefield established his Orphan House in Georgia, but it was supported by people in all of the Colonies. He did not solicit money for this institution during his first itinerary of the Middle Colonies but, when he went to New England, he began to take offerings for its support in every preaching service. He continued this practice until his death. His personal journal records the amounts received for the Orphan House day by day. This institution became the forerunner of many others like it in America.

The seeds of social reform were sown by the fervent preachers who were our Lord's witnesses in Colonial America. Whitefield attacked the abuse of slaves but not the institution of slavery. He also sought to establish schools for the Negroes. The time was not ripe for the institution of slavery to be brought to the bar of public opinion in America but this interest in the slaves was the seed that germinated and bore fruit in the abolition movement.

The rise of democracy in the New World was accelerated by the evangelism of the Colonial period. The common people were neglected, illiterate, and irreligious at the beginning of the eighteenth century. The evangelists of the era preached to the masses and the common man was redeemed. He was redeemed for eternity by the power of the Gospel, but he was also redeemed and made significant in his own day by this revival movement. The preaching of the New Side Presbyterians in the Middle Colonies and of the Baptists and the Methodists in the Southern Colonies reached and transformed thousands of the common people. The common man was thus led to see his own dignity and worth in the sight of God and, therefore, in the life of the nation which was soon to be.

The common people also were provided with an influential leadership from their own ranks by the evangelism of the later Colonial period. The New Side Presbyterian ministers who were trained by William Tennent in his famous Log College were from the ranks of the common people. These men established many other "Log Colleges" and were used of the Holy Spirit to recruit and train other leaders from the masses of the common people. The Baptist and Methodist preachers who won thousands to Christ in the Southern colonies were of the common people also. These men, though not educated in the schools, possessed splendid native abilities and a burning zeal. Some of them became influential in the affairs of the day as well as in evangelism. John Leland, a Baptist minister of Virginia, influenced the political philosophy of Thomas Jefferson to a marked degree, and the monthly business meetings of a small Baptist Church near Monticello impressed him as containing "the true principles of civil government."[2] This age of revivals produced leaders for the common people who could make the voice of the masses articulate. The will of the hitherto neglected people expressed through these leaders became potent in shaping the political structure of the infant nation.[3]

The Baptists and the Presbyterians, who led in the struggle for religious liberty and the separation of Church and State, became numerous through the revivals of the later Colonial period. Religious liberty, which is the mother of all other libertes, could not have been won without the large numbers of adherents to these two groups that bore the brunt of the battle. The influence of these humble masses who were willing to go to prison or to death for personal religious liberty was used in the providence of God to bring this priceless

---

2. Gewehr, *op. cit.,* p. 195.

3. "Among the Baptists of Virginia no one seems to have had more influence than John Leland. It is commonly maintained that it was Leland's withdrawal from the contest that assured Madison's election to the convention for the ratification of the constitution in Virginia." (Gewehr, *op. cit.,* p. 189)

"The business then (of the Baptists) was to unite as an oppressed people in using our influences and give our voice in electing members of the State legislature—members favorable to religious liberty and the rights of conscience." Wm. Fristoe, *History of the Ketocton Baptist Association,* Staunton, Va., 1808, p. 90. (*Ibid.* p. 194.)

boon to America. They appeared upon the American scene for such a time as this as a result of the fervent evangelism which preceded the war for independence.

The voice of these twice-born common people would not have been heard by the makers of the American nation but for the organizations which they developed during this time of revival. The protests against governmental regulation of the churches were made by Baptist Associations and Presbyterian Synods. Such memorials and petitions from individual churches would likely have been ignored, but when they came from organizations speaking for large numbers of churches and thousands of members, they won a hearing. The voice of the common people was heard through their denominational organizations.

Popular education received a new incentive and emphasis as a result of Colonial evangelism. The common people were aroused to the need of education for their children. The leaders in the revivals in the newer settlements established private schools where there were no public schools. The coming of universal popular education for American youth was hastened by these schools.

Christian education appeared in the very beginnings of the American Colonies. But the early colleges were primarily for the education of ministers. The schools which came into being as a result of the Great Awakening looked also to the training of the laity. The famous Log College which was established by William Tennent and perpetuated by the New Side Presbyterians became Princeton University. Liberty Hall Academy which was established in Virginia before the Revolution is now Washington and Lee University. Thus several denominational colleges which had their beginnings during the Great Awakening have grown to be great institutions of learning and have continued to the present time. Their contribution to the life of the nation cannot be evaluated.

One of the largest denominational publication societies in America, the Methodist Book Concern, had its beginnings in this perod of revival. Robert Williams, the first preacher to be sent to America by John Wesley, supplemented his preaching ministry by the publication of tracts and pamphlets. Sweet and Gewehr state that this was the seed from which grew the Methodist Book Concern—an institution of international influence at present.[4]

Finally, the evangelism of the Colonial period revived and established evangelical Christianity in America. It decided that American Christianity would be predominantly evangelical, experimental, and evangelistic rather than formal and liturgical. Humphrey says:

"After making every abatement, the years of the 'Great Awakening' were precious years of the right hand of the Most High. It left the churches of New England in a far sounder and better state than it found them. It effectually shut the door against admitting unregenerate persons to the Lord's supper as a converting ordinance, which Mr. Stoddard had unhappily opened in his own church, and by his writings in others. Reasoning out of the Scriptures, Mr. Edwards, in his 'Terms of Communion,' showed the practice to be wholly indefensible; and I am not aware that any evangelical church has favored it since. This was a great gain. Had the practice been continued, and become universal, it would have been more than a paralysis. The churches might have retained their names, but as true churches of Christ they would not have survived.

"Another important gain was, that the revival, widely extended and powerful as it was, prepared the way for freeing the churches from the 'Half-way Covenant.' Though in some quarters it held its ground longer, it was very much circumscribed. We shall meet with some remains of it hereafter, but dying out.

"Another immense gain to the cause of Christ was, that it greatly relieved the churches from the soporific influence of an unconverted ministry. It was admitted that there were unconverted pastors over some of the churches, and regeneration had come to be thought by many no essential qualifica-

4. *Ibid.*, p. 146.

tion for the sacred office. It was held, that if preachers were men of blameless lives they were not to be rejected though they did not profess to have been born again. Some of this number were the subjects of the revival, and confessed that they had preached for years without knowing what experimental piety was. In this respect the revival prepared the way for a great change for the better. It is not claimed that there can be any certain protection against the intrusion of unconverted men into the ministry. The strictest examination for the cure of souls cannot shut them out, for God alone knows the heart; but that none save converted men are fit to enter the ministry, is now universally held by the evangelical churches of all denominations.

"Moreover, the preaching in the orthodox churches has, ever since this great revival, been more spiritual and discriminating than it was when it began. The cardinal doctrines of universal and entire depravity. regeneration by the Holy Spirit, and justification by faith alone, with other kindred evangelical topics drawn from the word of God, held from that time forth a more prominent place in the ministrations of the pulpit, than they had done for ages before.

"Hence, though all that could have been desired was not accomplished, the good seed was sown broadcast over the land; and though we shall find, in the next period, that many hostile influences checked its growth for nearly half a century, it was so far from being lost where it did not spring up at once, that it was to take root and grow and ripen into other harvests, with more wheat, fewer tares, and less chaff."[5]

Humphrey's statement concerns the churches of New England only, but similar results appeared in all of the colonies. The evangelism of this era changed the course of the stream of Christianity for all of America. This is one reason for the predominantly evangelical Christianity in this country.

---

5. Humphrey, *op. cit.*, pp. 92-93.

DIVISION TWO

THE PERIOD OF NATIONAL BEGINNINGS 1775-1860

CHAPTER VIII

EVANGELISM IN THE AFTERMATH OF WAR

The American Revolution produced certain conditions in American Church life which hindered evangelism for several years after the war. There were divisions among the denominations based on the relationship of some of the Christian groups with England and the Church of England. The Anglicans and the Methodists were loyal to the mother Church and the mother country. The Anglican group was almost swept from the American scene by the victory of the colonists, and the Methodists, who were still a part of the Church of England, were seriously embarrassed. The Presbyterians, the Baptists and the Congregationalists supported the Revolution and were, therefore, in a better position to win the American people to Christ after the struggle for liberty was over.

There were also divisions within the denominations and in local churches. Most of the Methodist ministers returned to England at the outbreak of the war because they were loyal subjects of the crown and members of the Church of England. Others elected to remain in America and to support the colonies in their war of independence. There was a struggle between two loyalties in many of the local congregations of various denominations. The Quakers gave support to the English by their policy of non-resistance and some Baptists in the Southern colonies remained loyal to England because they were not sufficiently informed as to the causes of the war.[1] These divisions marred the fellowship of the churches and thus hindered evangelism.

The war had been promoted through the pulpits of the churches that were in sympathy with the colonists. The preachers had appealed for support of the Revolution as a "holy war." Some of them left their pulpits to join the army and to fight for freedom. Their passionate preaching and self-

1. Newman, A. H. A History of The Baptist Churches in The United States. The Christian Literature Co. New York, 1894   p. 376.

sacrifice may have been justified but they retarded evangelism by arousing hatred, producing division and diverting the attention of the people from the heart of the Gospel. The Presbyterian Synod of 1783 passed resolutions commending that group for "the general and almost universal attachment of the Presbyterian body to the cause of liberty," as confessed by the complaints and resentments of the common enemy."[2] During the war, the Reverend James Caldwell of this group brought an armful of psalm books to the soldiers to be used for wadding in their muskets.[3] The Baptists and the Congregationalists were as ardent in their support of the war as were the Presbyterians. Such activities produced an attitude not conducive to evangelization.

The British soldiers delighted to destroy and desecrate the houses of worship in which these groups met. When they captured an American town, they would seize the church buildings of those who were not loyal to Britain, to be used for barracks, hospitals or stables for their horses. When they moved on, they demolished these buildings. The Presbyterian Synod of 1783 complained of "our burnt and wasted Churches" as the result of these depredations. The American armies retaliated in kind. They seized, desecrated and demolished Anglican and Methodist buildings wherever they conquered. When the war was over, many congregations had no houses of worship, others gathered in buildings that were partly demolished, and still others were called to worship in buildings which had unholy associations with the war. When they met in these buildings, they were reminded of the hatred which had burned at white heat for seven years and which had caused the death of many whom they loved. This condition could not but hinder the work of evangelization.

Another problem of adjustment was a serious hindrance to aggressive evangelism in the year that immediately followed the war. The ecclesiastical connections of some of the religious groups with their forebears in England had to be

2. Thompson, R. E. *A History of The Presbyterian Churches in The United States*, Chas Scribner's Sons. New York, 1902. pp. 56-57.
3. *Ibid.*, p. 57

broken and replaced by organizations with no foreign alliances. This was accomplished speedily but the process consumed time and energy which might have been used in evangelization.

The alliance of the colonies with France brought French soldiers, seamen and civilians to almost every American port. Many of these Frenchmen were deists. Thompson says that "the frivolous and scoffing deism of the school of Voltaire was thus naturalized in America, and an irreligious tone began to pervade its society, especially its public life. Religion was valued, if at all, as a supplement to the jail and the police; belief in a disclosure of God to his creatures was thought a jestworthy superstition."[4]

Many of the Christian colleges were closed for the duration of the war and for some years after. This stopped the training of ministers and thus slowed the advance of evangelism. The college property which belonged to the various Christian groups received the same treatment from the armies that the Church buildings received. They became hospitals or barracks or barns according to the needs of the fighting men.

The tremendous struggle for religious freedom and the separation of Church and State which followed the war was another hindrance to the work of evangelism. The Anglican Church was the State Church in Virginia as was the Congregational Church in some of the New England colonies. These groups fought for a continuance of the status quo while the Baptists, the Presbyterians and others contended for absolute religious freedom and the complete separation of Church and State. The struggle was intense and bitter for years but the denominations that had supported the Revolution were victorious. This battle had to be fought but the energy it consumed and the enmity it generated were a hindrance to an aggressive evangelism.

The older colonies began to lose in population before the war because of the migration to the "new west." This migration was arrested by the Revolution but it was renewed on a larger scale after the treaty of peace was signed. This

4. *Ibid.*, p. 58.

unsettled condition was a detriment to evangelism for a few years but it prepared the soil for a great period of revival later.

In view of these facts and influences in American life, it is not surprising that the fifteen year period immediately following the war was "one of spiritual deadness among all the American Churches."[5] One writer describes these years as "the period of lowest ebb-tide in the history of American Christianity."[6] Dr. Sweet says that, "There were numerous Jacobin clubs and societies of the Illuminati throughout the country, directing their energy to the ridicule of Christianity and the bringing in of the Age of Reason."[7]

Lyman Beecher was a student at Yale in 1795. In his Reminiscences, he describes the college as follows:

"The College was in a most ungodly state. The College Church was almost extinct. Most of the students were skeptical, and rowdies were plenty. Wine and liquors were kept in many rooms; intemperance, profanity, gambling and licentiousness in common."[8]

The students in college would address each other as Rosseau or Voltaire and would boast of their infidelity. A common subject for debate was: "Whether Christianity had been beneficial or injurious to mankind."

These were dark days for evangelism and evangelical Christianity but the darkness did not extinguish the light in all parts of America. There were local revivals in the newer states and a general revival in Virginia even during these years. Dr. Newman, the Baptist historian, speaks of a revival in Kentucky in 1785 which, "resulted in the formation of nine additional churches."[9] But he says that the years from 1793 to 1800 were "a period of spiritual dearth" and that "infidelity and immorality increased at an alarming rate in the state."

Virginia was the only state to be visited by a general revival during these years. Three denominations, Methodists,

5. Sweet, W. W., *The Story of Religions in America*, Harper and Brothers, New York, 1939. p. 322.
6. *Loc. Cit.*
7. *Loc. Cit.*
8. *Ibid.*, p. 323.
9. Newman, A. H., *A History of the Baptist Churches in The United States*. The Christian Literature Co. New York. 1902 p. 334.

Baptists and Presbyterians, serving the entire state were blessed with a remarkable visitation of God's power. This movement reached high-tide from 1787 to 1789.

The Methodist revival began in 1785 in southeastern Virginia. It reached its peak by the spring of 1788. It is surprising that this group could be used of the Holy Spirit with such effectiveness at this early date after the war. Their old world connections had hindered them greatly during the war but their societies were firmly established in this section of Virginia. Their zeal, their insistence upon a vital personal religious experience and their hymns met the needs of the hour and they were blessed with a great revival.

This revival, according to Jesse Lee, a Methodist historian of the period, was greater than the one which had been stopped by the war. Mr. Lee wrote: "Such a time for awakening and conversion of sinners was never before seen among the Methodists in America."[10] Many of the people thought that everybody would surely be converted in this movement. People neglected their crops in attending the meetings to such an extent that there was a fear that they would not harvest enough for bare necessities, but "the crops were tolerably good."

The power of this Methodist revival is shown by the large number of conversions. A quarterly meeting was held at Mabry's chapel in July, 1787. There were one hundred and fifty conversions on the first day and on the second day, "above a hundred whites found peace with God, besides as many negroes."[11] An eye witness reports that perhaps four thousand people attended this meeting. A little later in the summer, another quarterly meeting was held at Jones' Chapel where the crowds were larger and the conversions more numerous. Garretson says that he preached to more than fifteen hundred people in the woods during the Jones' Chapel meeting while other preachers were preaching in the church building and in a nearby barn. There were more than four thousand conversions in the three largest circuits of Virginia within one year.

10. Gewehr, W. M. *The Great Awakening in Virginia.* Duke University Press. Durham. N. C. 1930. p. 168.
11. *Ibid.*, p. 169.

The emotional excesses which appeared in these meetings were more extreme than those of the previous Methodist revivals. In the quarterly meeting at Jones' Chapel, the shouts of the people could be heard a half-mile from the building even before the preachers arrived. When the preachers appeared on the scene, there were about sixty people on the floor, "groaning in loud cries to God for mercy." The preachers could not make themselves heard because of the cries of the distressed. One of them wrote, "Such a sight, I never had seen before; numbers of saints in ecstasies, others crying for mercy, scores lying with their eyes set in their heads, the use of their powers suspended, and the whole congregation in agitation."[12]

Such scenes as the one described above appeared in many of the Methodist meetings of this period. The crowds became so large that meetings had to be held in the open. Many entire families were won to Christ and the new converts would often begin to exhort others with great effectiveness. These testimonies and exhortations helped to win others and to promote the revival.

The movement began to wane in the spring of 1788 and the Methodist Societies did not experience other awakenings until the close of the century. The fact that such large numbers had been converted in a sparsely settled area and that the emotional excesses had been so extreme likely contributed to the decline.

The Baptists, because of their sympathy with the Revolution and their lack of old world connections, were in better position to evangelize the citizens of the infant nation than were the Methodists. An evangelistic movement appeared among this group in northern Virginia in 1785. It reached its height in 1787 to 1789 but continued with considerable force until 1792. Available statistics are meager but a glimpse at the records of a few of the churches reveals that there were thousands of conversions. For example, the Nomini Church was organized in April, 1786, with seventeen members. By the end of the year, there were seventy-three

12. *Ibid.*, p. 170.

members. The letters to the Association reported 222 members in 1788 and 300 in 1789. By 1792, thousands had been added to the churches and, "Their congregations became more numerous than those of any other Christian sect." Many of the leading citizens had become Baptist by this time.

Extreme emotional manifestations appeared in the Baptist meetings also. A Baptist historian of this period says: "It was not unusual to have a large proportion of a congregation prostrate on the floor; and, in some instances, they have lost the use of their limbs. No distinct articulation could be heard unless from those immediately by. Screams, cries, groans, songs, shouts and hozannas, notes of grief and notes of joy, all heard at the same time, made a heavenly confusion, a sort of indescribable concert. Even the wicked and unenlighted were astonished and said, 'the Lord hath done great things for his people.' At associations and great meetings, where there were several ministers, many of them would exercise their gifts at the same time in different parts of the congregation; some in exhortation, some in praying for the distressed; and some in argument with the opposers."[13]

This same historian also says that there were many spurious conversions in these meetings. He says that, "there was a little confusion and disorder" in some of the Churches after the revival had subsided, and that, "Some of the ministers who labored earnestly to get Christians into their Churches were afterwards much perplexed to get out hypocrites."[14]

NOTE:

This quotation is the first reference to "hypocrites" or spurious conversions which the author has found in the research incident to writing this book. The enemies of the revivals of the Great Awakening era raised the question as to whether persons who had been totally indifferent to religion could be converted instantly but this statement about getting "hypocrites" out of the churches was made by friends of evangelism. The promoters of the revivals in Colonial America seem to have been convinced that every conversion was a genuine work of God. The fact that the Methodists received new converts as "probationers" for a time before they became full members of the societies did not spring from the fact that Methodist leaders doubted the genuineness of the conversion experience. They wanted to be sure that the new convert would "go on to perfection."

13. *Ibid.*, p. 176.
14. *Ibid.*, p. 177.

Baptists grew in numbers in all parts of America from the close of the war to the end of the century but evangelism did not produce all of the growth. In New England and the Middle Colonies, many people left other Churches and joined the Baptists because of doctrinal teachings. In the newer states, the growth may be explained largely by immigration although there were local revivals of consequence. There was no wide-spread evangelistic movement in any other state, however, like the one in Virginia.

There was a thorough-going revival among the Presbyterians in southeastern Virginia from 1787 to 1789. It began in Hampden-Sidney College when Gary Allen, a student, was converted. He and a few other students began to hold prayer meetings in the College to the very great surprise of the student body. When the young men returned to their homes for the vacation period, they took the zeal of the revival with them and it spread over several counties in Virginia and even into North Carolina.

The leading preacher among the Presbyterians during this season of revival was John Blair Smith, President of Hampden-Sidney. He encouraged Gary Allen and the other students. He began to preach with more zeal in his own pulpit and to promote prayer meetings in the community. His preaching has been described as follows: "The truth of God was preached plainly, and with reference to an immediate effect. The total depravity of man, his responsibility and guilt, the necessity of repentance and faith in Jesus Christ, the dependence of the sinner upon the Spirit of God, and the retribution of eternity, were the great truths exhibited during this season of revivals."[15]

The Reverend Robert Smith, father of President John Blair Smith, described this revival among the Presbyterians in a letter written in October 1788, as follows:

"I have seen nothing equal to it for extensive spread, power and spiritual glory since the years of '40 and '41. The work has spread for an hundred miles, but by far the most powerful and general in John Smith's congregations, which

15. *Ibid.*, p. 179.

take in part of three counties. Not a word scarcely about politics; but all religion in public and private. They run far and near to sermons, sacraments and societies, which meet every Wednesday and Saturday evenings, and at College on Sabbath evenings, also. Numbers of the students have been convinced and several of them hopefully converted . . . The blessed work has spread among people of every description, high and low, rich and poor, learned and unlearned, orthodox and heterodox, sober and rude, white and black, young and old; especially the youth, whom it seems to have seized generally. Two hundred and twenty-five hopeful communicants have been added to the Lord's table among John Smith's people in the space of eighteen months chiefly of the young people."[16]

The Presbyterian revival was different from those of the Methodists and the Baptists in that there were no extreme emotional demonstrations. These would have appeared but for the influence of John Blair Smith who would stop in the midst of a sermon to remind the people that God is not the author of confusion. He often had to restrain the people to prevent the outbreak similar to the unbridled expression which was given to emotion in the other meetings of the period.

The Presbyterian Church in Virginia was revitalized by this brief period of revival. The spirit of evangelism had almost vanished from this group but it returned with vigor to prepare the Church for a great growth in the South.

From the close of the Revolution to the end of the century, religion was at low-tide in most of America. The only exception to this statement was the brief period of revival in Virginia. These years were characterized by a great migration to the "new west," the spread of deism and immorality over the nation. This condition obtained when the Great Awakening of 1800 came to bless and to revitalize American Christianity.

16. *Ibid.*, p. 180.

CHAPTER IX

THE PERIOD OF NATIONAL UNITY—1790-1830

The Methodist, Presbyterian, and Baptist revivals in Virginia during the first decade after the War for Independence subsided by 1792. They were followed by a period of spiritual decadence in this section and in these denominations. The churches of the eastern states witnessed no revivals after the war until 1791, when local revivals began among the Congregationalists of New England. Thus there was a spiritual awakening in Virginia during the first few years after the war, followed by a decade of declension. In the east, there was a decade of spiritual barrenness followed by ten years of spiritual awakening by the end of the century.

The earliest of these local revivals came to the Congregational churches of New England. They began quietly in North Yarmouth, Maine, in 1791 and spread over most of New England by the end of the century. Dr. Edward D. Griffin, pastor at New Hartford, Connecticut, wrote in 1799:

"I saw a continual succession of heavenly sprinklings . . . in Connecticut until I could stand at my door in New Hartford . . . and number fifty or sixty contiguous congregations laid down in one field of divine wonders, and as many more in different parts of New England."[1]

These revivals were conducted by local pastors, there being no outstanding evangelists traveling from church to church. These awakenings spread quietly and powerfully in all parts of New England. They seemed to gain momentum with the passing of the years for two generations.[2]

Presbyterian Churches in western New England witnessed similar local revivals beginning in 1792. Moral and religious conditions in these commmunities had been deplorable

1. Walker, W. A History of The Congregational Churches in The United States. Chas. Scribner's Sons. N. Y. 1902. p. 319,
2. Ibid., p. 320.

77

since the beginning of the war for independence. A Presbyterian historian, (Thompson) says:

"From the close of the war for independence spiritual influences appeared to lose their hold on the popular mind. Unbelief became the fashion of the day. There was a decay of zeal in the churches, and in the eastern part of Massachusetts a rapid spread of socianism. The first signs of a change came in 1792 when extensive revivals occurred, especially in western New England."

These revivals, like those among the Congregationalists, were conducted by local pastors. They were used of the Holy Spirit to win men for Christ, raise moral standards and check the spread of deism among the common people.

There were not many Methodists in New England when this period of spiritual awakening opened. Yet their evangelistic fervor fitted them well to share in it and to promote it throughout the infant nation. A revival occured in the General Conference during its meeting in Baltimore in 1797. From this conference, it spread through the Methodist Societies of the eastern states. A Methodist historian says:

"As the preachers returned to their stations they naturally carried the influence of this revival and lighted similar flames wherever they went. In and near the place where was held the first Annual Conference after the adjournment of the General Conference, not far from Baltimore, within a few days one hundred and seventeen joined the Society."[3]

These revivals in the three major denominations seem to have reached the common people only. Members of the "better families" were skeptics in large numbers as late as 1796. There was only one "professing Christian" among the freshmen who entered Yale College that year. There was none in the sophomore class and only one in the junior class. The senior class included eight or ten, making a total of not more than a dozen in the entire student body. In 1795, when

3. Buckley, J. M. *A History of Methodists in The United States.* Chas. Scribner's Sons. New York, 1902. pp. 297-8.

Timothy Dwight came to Yale as president, only two students would confess that they believed in God.[4]

The morals of college groups were at an extremely low level during the closing years of the century. Lyman Beecher, who was a student in Yale College in 1795 describes conditions there as follows: "Most of the students were skeptical, and rowdies were plenty. Wine and liquors were kept in many rooms; intemperance, profanity, gambling and licentiousness were common."[5]

Conditions similar to those at Yale appeared on other campuses. Princeton was a Presbyterian school, but in 1782 there were only two students who professed to be Christians.[6] The General Assembly, meeting in 1798, published the following description of theological thought and public morals:

"We note with pain and fearful apprehension a general dereliction of religious principles and practice among our fellow-citizens, a visible and prevailing impiety and contempt for the laws and institutions of religion, and an abounding infidelity, which in many cases tends to atheism itself. The profligacy and corruption of the public morals have advanced with a progress proportionate to our declension in religion. Profaneness, pride, luxury, injustice, intemperance, lewdness, and every species of debauchery and loose indulgences greatly abound."[7]

For such a time as this, God raised up Timothy Dwight, a grandson of Jonathan Edwards. He inherited much of the mental acumen of his famous grandfather and was taught Edwardean theology and Puritan morals by his mother. Being a precocious child, he advanced in the classical studies of his day. Before entering Yale College in 1765, he had completed the courses of study offered there for the first and second years. After his graduation, he served as a tutor in Yale for eight years, resigning that position to become a chaplain

4. Cunningham, C. E. *Timothy Dwight, a Biography.* The MacMillan Company. N. Y. 1942. p. 302.
5. Sweet, W. W. *The Story of Religions in America.* Harper and Brothers. New York. 1942. p. 323.
6. *Ibid.,* p. 324.
7. *Loc. Cit.*

in Washington's army.   His service in the chaplaincy brought
the young clergyman into close contact with the gross immorality usually associated with war and with French deism.
A pastorate of twelve years at Greenfield Hill, a rural parish,
gave him further time for study and thought upon the issues
of the hour. He conceived of deism, which had been brought
to America by French statesmen and soldiers during the war,
as a great danger to the life of the infant nation.   He had
already begun to fight this menace before he was chosen as
president of Yale in 1795.

The students seem to have felt that the battle would soon
be joined when Dwight assumed the responsibilities of the
presidency.   They were very certain that Christianity was a
dead issue in that "Age of Reason."   The seniors seized their
first opportunity to test the new president.   In the list of possible topics to be discussed before him,   they submitted the
following question: "Are the Scriptures of the Old Testament and the New Testament the Word of God?" Dwight
chose this question for the first "disputation," permitting the
members of the class to take either side in the debate. Cunningham says: "Here was an opportunity they never dreamed
would be given them.   They must make the most of it. When
the day for the dispute came, most, if not all came forward as
champions of infidelity. Dwight allowed each to state his case
fully."[8]

When the seniors had presented their arguments, President Dwight entered the debate personally.   He showed them
how little they knew about the subject and that many of their
statements of fact were either mistaken or irrelevant.   He
then presented proof of the divine origin of the Scriptures
with irresistable logic and commanding eloquence. His biographer says that Dwight's handling of the question "left the
stoutest infidel utterly confounded. His bolts had the effect
of lightning on the whole college."[9]

The new president followed this first encounter with   a
series of sermons in the chapel on, "The Unreasonableness of

8. Cunningham, C. E. *Timothy Dwight, a Biography*. The MacMillan
   Company. N. Y. 1942. pp. 300-1.
9. *Ibid.*, p. 301.

Infidelity." Soon he preached a second series on "Theology Explained and Defended," and a third on, "The Nature and Danger of the Infidel Philosophy." This was followed by another on, "Is the Bible the Word of God?"[10]

His preaching was a convincing answer on the intellectual plane to the scoffing deism of the day. His own conversion experience was a laboratory demonstration of the fact that God does enter into the experiences of men. The Holy Spirit used this man and his message to bring a religious awakening to the campus in 1802. One third of the students were converted and more than thirty of the new converts became ministers. This awakening began when some young men who had been converted in local revivals came to Yale.

This wave of evangelism brought a marked moral reformation to the campus. A student who was influenced by it said that the college was changed from "a sink of moral and spiritual pollution into a residence not only of science and literature, but of morality and religion, a nursery for piety and virtue, a fountain from which has issued streams to make glad the city of God."[11] The moral reformation in this college community was quite as remarkable as the reformation in the village of Northampton two generations earlier under the preaching of Jonathan Edwards.

Other visitations of God's power came to Yale during the first quarter of the nineteenth century. During the remaining years of Dwight's presidency one-fourth to one-third of the students were members of the College Church. Many others who could not relate a conversion experience regulated their lives according to Christian standards. Other colleges in the east, such as Williams, Amherst, and Dartmouth, enjoyed similar seasons of revival during the first three decades of the nineteenth century.

The rank and file of the population was blessed through the local revivals which began in the east in 1791. The col-

10. Sweet, W. W. *The Story of Religions in America*. Harper and Brothers. N. Y. 1939. p. 326.
11. Cunningham, C. E., *Timothy Dwight, a Biography*. The MacMillan Company. N. Y. 1942. p. 303.

lege groups were transformed by the awakenings which began in Yale in 1802. Infidelity had been routed and Christianity was militant and triumphant. The growth of Church membership continued to outstrip the growth of the population during these four decades—from 5% in 1790 to 13.3% in 1830.

The revival fires moved westward with the immigrants who poured into the "new west" in large numbers. Congregationalism spread into Vermont, the first territory to the west, so rapidly that there were seventy-four churches in that area by 1800. The rapidly expanding frontier was a challenge to evangelistic and missionary zeal in the Congregational Church. Ohio was admitted to the Union in 1803, but a Congregational church had been organized in the territory seven years prior to that date. It was called, "Old Northwest."

The Congregationalists did not move far into the "new west," because of an agreement with the Presbyterians. The Presbyterians were effective evangelists on the frontier during the first thirty years of the nineteenth century. The first appearance of the revival among the Presbyterians in the "new west" was in 1798 in the Red River Valley of Kentucky.

Interest in religion had been so lacking in Kentucky that the legislature, meeting in 1793, voted to dispense with the prayers in its sessions. But James McGready, who had been converted under the fervent preaching of "Log College" men and trained by them, came to live in the Red River Valley. His personal appearance has been described as "exceedingly uncouth." His preaching was searching, like the powerful preaching of Gilbert Tennent of "Great Awakening" fame. He had preached in North and South Carolina as early as 1796. Here he had been accused of "running the young people distracted"[13] with his lurid word pictures of the doom of sinners.

Mr. McGready was the preacher for the frontier in such a time as this. The common people were hungry for the Word of God. The easterner who had left his settled community

13. Sweet, p. 328.

where preaching was easily available may have neglected it there, but his heart soon hungered for it on the frontier where preachers and preaching were scarce. A Presbyterian historian says: "The hunger for preaching went far beyond the power of the ministers to meet it. Laymen, even children were heard eagerly and with powerful effect."[14] To these hungry-hearted settlers came McGready with a burning zeal. His fervor in depicting the horrible consequences of sin disturbed the consciences of those who were guilty of the gross sins of the frontier. His own personal conversion experience was another demonstration that God does enter into human experience. This refuted any deistic thinking which may have appeared on the border of the rapidly expanding nation.

Under the preaching of McGready the great Cumberland revival began in 1798 and continued with increasing power for some three years. The crowds were soon so large that meetings had to be held in the fields, just as in the days when George Whitefield and Gilbert Tennent preached. People came in wagons, on horseback, and on foot for miles and camped on the scene that they might attend the meetings. It was here that the famous "Camp Meeting" came into the life of the American frontier. It played an important role in the evangelization of this and the next generation. This revival, with the camp meetings and earnest preaching spread throughout all the border settlements. The meetings were either denominational or interdenominational, appearing in Baptist and Methodist groups as well as among the Presbyterians.

From 1792, when the Baptist revival in Virginia subsided, until 1801, evangelism was at low tide among the Baptists. In the beginning of the nineteenth century, three ministers appeared in Georgia who were destined to influence Georgia Baptists in the fields of education, missions and evangelism. They were Henry Holcombe, Jesse Mercer, and Joseph Clay. They were not outstanding evangelists but the educational institutions which they fostered and the missionary

14. Thompson, A. E. *A History of The Presbyterian Churches in The United States.* Chas. Scribner's Sons. N. Y. 1902. p. 74

organizations which they inaugurated gave a new impetus to evangelism. All three of these men did evanglistic work but their major contributions were in the other two fields.

Holcombe was a young cavalry officer when he was converted in 1784. He was ordained in 1785 and became pastor of the newly-organized church in Savannah, Georgia, in 1800. The membership of this church increased from ten to sixty in two years.

Jesse Mercer was a pioneer in Christian education and in missionary organization. The sustaining passion of his life, however, was the desire to win men to Christ. When he was baptized by his father in 1787, he "began almost immediately to labor for the salvation of souls."[15] Being an educator and a missionary statesman, Mercer has God's man to launch evangelistic crusade with a world-wide outlook and a passion to educate and enlist the evangelized.

Judge Joseph Clay was converted to the views of the Baptists by the preaching of Henry Holcombe. He left a high judicial position to become a Baptist minister. He was licensed to preach in 1802 and ordained in 1804. He brought into the ministry a trained legal mind just as a new day for evangelism was beginning to dawn in Georgia.

The first twelve years of the new century were a period of effective evangelism among the Negroes of Georgia. Negro ministers became prominent and influential. In 1810, the population of Georgia was 252,432, including 145,414 slaves. A number of large Negro churches had grown up under the leadership of pastors of their own race. These Negro ministers received much encouragement from their white brethren. There were also many Negro members in the white churches. The influence of one Negro pastor and his effectiveness as an evangelist are revealed by a resolution passed by the Savannah Association (White) in 1812. The resolution stated:

"The Association is sensibly affected by the death of the Rev. Andrew Bryan, a man of color and pastor of the first

15. **Newman, A. H.** *A History of The Baptist Churches in The United States.* The Christian Literature Co. N. Y. 1894. p. 322

colored church in Savannah. This son of Africa, after suffering inexpressible persecutions in the cause of his divine Master, was at length permitted to discharge the duties of the ministry among his colored friends, hundreds of whom through his instrumentality, were brought to a knowledge of the truth as it is in Jesus. He closed his extensively useful and amazingly luminous course in the lively exercise of faith, and in the joyful hope of a happy immortality."[16]

This resolution, written and adopted by his white brethren, states that this Negro minister won many of his race to Christ. Other Negro ministers, like Andrew Marshall of Savannah and Jacob Walker of Augusta, were also effective evangelists.

Newman says: "The period closed (1800-1812) in the midst of one of the greatest religious awakenings ever known in Georgia. Nearly all of the Baptist pastors turned evangelists, and with wonderful enthusiasm covered the State with their missionary activity. Churches were springing up everywhere."

There were 428 Baptists in Georgia in 1784. Their numbers had increased to 15,755 by 1813.

Baptists moved into the frontier states in great numbers between 1800 and 1812. The farmer-preacher came in search of better land. He was especially adapted to the frontier settler because he was of the common people and was able to speak their language. These earnest preachers won thousands to Christ. Their effectiveness is revealed by the following statistics:

In 1792 there were forty-two Baptist churches in Kentucky with a total membership of 3,095. There were 285 churches with a membership of 22,694 in 1812. There were only 21 churches with a membership of 900 in Tennessee in 1792, but they increased to 156 churches with a membership of 11,325 by 1812. Indiana had only two Baptist churches with a membership of 64 in 1790, but in 1812 there were 60

16. *Ibid.*, p. 331.

churches with a membership of 2400. There were only four churches in Illinois as late as 1807, but there were seven churches with a membership of 153 in 1812. The first Baptist church in Missouri was Bethel, organized in 1806. In 1812 there were seven Baptist churches in Missouri with a membership of 153.

The Methodists were on the scene in Kentucky when the great Cumberland revival began. They cooperated with the Presbyterians and others in "Camp Meetings." In 1799 and 1800, two brothers—John and William McGee—toured the settlements of Kentucky. John McGee was a Methodist; his brother was a Presbyterian. Vast throngs attended their meetings and thousands were converted. Methodist work was hindered by the war of 1812[17] but at the death of Bishop Asbury, in 1816, they numbered more than two hundred thousand in the United States.[18]

The zeal and devotion of the Methodist "Circuit Rider" were blessed of his Lord in winning many to Christ. The Methodist movement made its way into the remotest settlements of the frontier through the itinerant ministry of these earnest men. They were all traveling evangelists. The pastoral work in Methodism of that day was done by class leaders and local preachers. The following description of the labors of Bishop Asbury reveals both the methods and the spirit of these evangelists:

"Although never robust and often ill, he had no fixed home and travelled incessantly. Armed by his faith and spurred by his mission, he was undaunted by the hardships and perils of itineracy in the roughest sections of the new land. He ranged over the older states and through the crude settlements of the frontier. From Maine to Georgia and from the Atlantic seaboard to Kentucky, Ohio and Tennessee he went, largely on horseback. He inspired and supervised the circuit riders."[19]

17. Buckley, J. M. *A History of Methodists in The United States*. Chas. Scribner's Sons. N. Y. 1902.
18. Latourette, K. S., *A History of The Expansion of Christianity*. Vol. IV Harper and Brothers. N. Y. 1941. p. 188.
19. *Ibid.*, p. 187-88.

Thus a tidal wave of vital evangelism swept over the country from the older states of the east to the scattered settlements of the frontier during the first three decades of the nineteenth century. The population was increasing very rapidly during this period but the membership of the churches increased much more rapidly.

There were no emotional demonstrations in the east comparable to those of the Great Awakening. In the revivals of the frontier settlements, however, emotional excesses appeared which were even more violent than those of the Great Awakening era. Peter Cartwright, the famous camp-meeting evangelist of the Methodist Episcopal Church, described these outbursts of emotion as follows:

"I have seen more than a hundred sinners fall like dead men under one powerful sermon, and I have seen and heard more than five hundred Christians all shouting aloud the high praises of God at once; and I will venture to assert that many happy thousands were awakened and converted to God at these camp meetings.[20]

"The Presbyterian preachers and members, not being accustomed to much noise and shouting, when they yielded to it went into great extremes and downright wildness."

"Just in the midst of our controversies, on the subject of the powerful exercises among the people under preaching, a new exercise broke out among us, called the jerks, which was overwhelming in its effects upon the bodies and minds of the people. No matter whether they were saints or sinners, they would be taken under a warm song or sermon, and seized with a convulsive jerking all over, which they could not by any possibility avoid, and the more they resisted the more they jerked. If they would not strive against it and pray in good earnest, the jerking would usually abate. I have seen more than five hundred persons jerking at one time in my large congregations. Most usually persons taken with the jerks, to obtain relief as they said, would rise up and dance.

20. *Autobiography of Peter Cartwright*, Cincinnati, Cranston and Curts, 1856, pp. 46, 48-51. ·

Some would run, but could not get away. Some would resist; on such the jerks were generally very severe.

"To see those proud young gentlemen and young ladies, dressed in their silks, jewelry and prunella, from top to toe, take the jerks, would often excite my risibilities. The first jerk or so, you would see their fine bonnets, caps and combs fly; and so sudden would be the jerking of the head that their long loose hair would crack almost as loud as a wagoner's whip."[21]

"While I am on this subject I will relate a very serious circumstance which I knew to take place with a man who had the jerks at a camp meeting, on what was called the Ridge, in William Magee's congregation. There was a great work of religion in the encampment. The jerks were very prevalent. There was a company of drunken rowdies who came to interrupt the meeting. These rowdies were headed by a very large drinking man. They came with their bottles of whisky in their pockets. This large man cursed the jerks and all religion. Shortly afterwards he took the jerks, and he started to run, but he jerked so powerfully he could not get away. He halted among some saplings, and although he was violently agitated, he took out his bottle of whisky, and swore he would drink the damned jerks to death; but he jerked at such a rate he could not get the bottle to his mouth, though he tried hard. At length he fetched a sudden jerk, and the bottle struck a sapling and was broken to pieces, and spilled his whisky on the ground. There was a great crowd gathered around him, and when he lost his whisky he became very much enraged, and cursed and swore very profanely, his jerks still increasing. At length he fetched a very violent jerk, snapped his neck, fell and soon expired, with his mouth full of cursing and bitterness."[22]

"There were many other strange and wild exercises into which the subjects of the revival fell; such, for instance, as what was called the running, jumping and barking exercise."[23]

21. *Ibid.* pp. 48-49.
22. *Ibid.* pp. 50-51.
23. *Ibid.* p. 51

It is interesting to note that violent emotional demonstrations appeared in the camp meeting revival of the frontier but did not appear in the east. They did not appear on the eastern seaboard because there was a settled society there and most of the communities were losing in population because of the great westward migration. The revivals were local and in the churches. They did not attract the vast throngs like the camp meetings did in the "new west." There were no stirring orators like Jonathan Edwards, George Whitefield and Gilbert Tennent. The preaching was done by pastors whose fame did not spread far beyond the borders of their own parishes. The preaching in the college revivals was done by men like Timothy Dwight who were intellectual giants. Dwight attacked deism on the intellectual plane rather than the emotional. Furthermore, the love, zeal and enthusiasm aroused in these revivals found expression in mission work on the frontier. The Home Missions enterprise in the United States came into being during this period of religious awakenings.

Violent emotional demonstrations came to the frontier revivals for obvious reasons. The lonely pioneer was not accustomed to being in large crowds until the camp meetings came. When excitement appeared in a throng of such men and women, it spread rapidly and gained momentum. The emotions of the pioneer were stirred much more easily than the inhabitants of a more settled society. He had not learned to control his emotions as had his cousin in the older settlements of the east. The man who was used of the Lord to start the great Cumberland revival was McGready—a historical and a theological descendent of the Tennents and the "New Side" Presbyterians. It was the preaching of these "New Side" Presbyterians, trained in the famous "Log Colleges," that often produced excesses in the Great Awakening. The Methodist movement was characterized by much emotion from its beginning. Their background fitted them to share in the outbursts of emotion which appeared in the camp meetings. The Baptist preachers of this period were the historical and theological descendants of Shubal Stearns, John Marshall and the "Separate Baptists." They had a tradition of unbridled expression of the emotions.

There was a slight recession in evangelism at the time of the war of 1812 but it did not slow the evangelistic advance very much. This was a great era of evangelism. The camp meeting made its appearance here and was used of the Lord as an effective agency in the spread of the gospel in the growing nation.

CHAPTER X

EVANGELISM IN THE WORLD FIELD—THE RISE OF HOME MISSIONS

The period of revival which came to the United States during the first three decades of the nineteenth century was just one phase of a world-wide movement. The explorations of the fifteenth and sixteenth centuries had enlarged the horizons of the entire world. Christian churches and their leaders shared these enlarged horizons. The discovery of pagan peoples and the establishment of colonies in remote sections of the earth had aroused the missionary and evangelistic zeal of Christians in Europe and had led to the organization of missionary movements.

The eighteenth century had witnessed the organization of many missionary societies in Europe. As early as 1701 the Church of England had organized the "Society for the Propagation of the Gospel" for the purpose of evangelizing the British colonists in foreign lands[1]. Danish Christians opened a mission in India in 1706.[2] British Baptists organized "The Baptist Society for the Propagation of the Gospel among the Heathen" at Kettering, England, on October second, 1792. They sent Carey and Thomas to India in 1793. The London Missionary Society came into being in 1795. This Church of England organization sought to evangelize the natives as well as the English colonists in foreign lands. They sent Robert Moffat to Africa in 1816 and David Livingstone in 1840.[3]

News of the sailing of Carey and Thomas reached America early in the nineteenth century and elicited the support of American Christians. In 1807, Congregationalists and Pres-

1. Vedder, H. C. *A Short History of Baptist Missions*, The Judson Press, Phil. Pa. 1925.
2. *Loc. Cit.*
3. Walker, W. *A History of the Congregational Churches in The United States.* Chas. Scribner's Sons. N. Y. 1902. p. 362

byterians in this county sent six thousand dollars to the
Carey mission in India. The Congregationalists formed "The
American Board of Commissioners for Foreign Missions" in
1810. This first foreign mission board in America sent missionaries to India in 1812. The Baptists organized "The General Missionary Convention of the Baptist Denomination in
the United States for Foreign Missions" in 1814 to assume the
support of the Judsons and Luther Rice in Burma.

It was in this setting of world-wide missionary interest
and effort that American Home Mission movements were
born. The rise of home mission organizations in America,
however, was preceded by a decade of gracious revivals. There
were vital and powerful local revivals among Congregational
churches in New England from 1791 to 1799. It was in 1798
that the General Association of Connecticut (Congregational)
organized itself into a Missionary Society "To Christianize the
Heathen in North America, and to support and promote Christian knowledge in the new settlements within the United
States."[4]

This first Home Missions organization in the United
States was a local society. The time for nation-wide movements had not arrived but local missionary societies sprang
up all along the eastern seaboard. In Massachusetts, the
"Congregational Missionary Society in the Counties of Berk-
shire and Columbia" appeared in 1798 and was followed the
next year by the "Massachusetts Missionary Society."
In 1801, "The New Hampshire Missionary Society"
and the "Boston Female Society for Missionary Purposes"
came into being. In 1804, the "Female Cent Society"
appeared in Boston and was organized. In the same year
the General Convention of Vermont began acting as a
missionary society.[5] The appearance of numerous other
local organizations for missionary purposes on the American
scene during the early years of the century reveals the missionary and evangelistic zeal of the churches.

4. *Ibid.* p. 312.
5. *Ibid.,* p. 313.

A vast amount of missionary literature was created by the rising tide of missions and evangelism. The appearance of missionary magazines stimulated and sustained the zeal of the churches by disseminating information about the needs of the fields and the triumphs of the gospel. The Congregationalists began the publication of the "Massachusetts Missionary Magazine" in 1803. The "Connecticut Bible Society" appeared in 1808 and the "Massachusetts Bible Society" the following year.[6] The Presbyterians established "The American Bible Society" in 1819 and "The American Tract Society" in 1825.

The publication of Baptist missionary literature and the organization of Baptists for mission work began in the early years of the nineteenth century. "The Analytical Repository" appeared in 1801 and was discontinued in 1802 for lack of financial support. Henry Holcombe was the editor. "The Massachusetts Missionary Magazine" which began publication in 1803 became "The Baptist Missionary Magazine" in 1826. The title was changed when that periodical became the organ of the Triennial Convention. News of the Carey mission in India along with the American Baptist mission in Burma appeared regularly in this magazine. It also carried news of missions in America and championed the cause of home missions.[7] Other Baptist periodicals had their beginnings in this era. "The Literary Luminary" and the "Columbian Star" appeared in 1822 as a result of the work of Luther Rice. "The Watchman" appeared in 1819, "The Western Recorder" in 1835, "The Baptist" in 1836, "Zion's Advocate" in 1828 and "The Christian Review" in 1836.

The publication of a literature separate from the periodicals was begun by the Baptists with the organization of "The Baptist General Tract Society" in 1824. Its purpose was to give publicity to Baptist doctrines as well as Baptist missions and to defend the doctrines. "The American and Foreign Bible Society" was organized in 1836 to translate the Scrip-

---

6. *Loc. Cit.*

7. Newman, A. H. *A History of The Baptist Churches in The United States.* The Christian Literature Co. N. Y. 1894. p. 384.

tures into foreign languages and to distribute Bibles and other religious literature in America.

Baptist periodicals and Baptist organizations for mission work appeared at the same time. Baptist women were members of the "Female Cent Society for Missionary purposes." This movement led to the organization of many "Cent Societies" in Baptist churches. "The Massachusetts Domestic Missionary Society" was organized in 1802, "To furnish occasional preacing and to promote the knowledge of evangelical truth in the new settlements; and further, if circumstances should render it proper." "The Lake Missionary Society" was organized at Pompey, New York, in 1807. It became "The Hamilton Missionary Society" in 1809. "The Baptist Society for the Propagation of the Gospel in Foreign Parts" was formed in Boston in 1813 when news of the conversions of the Judsons and Luther Rice to Baptist views reached that city. Many female societies appeared with special zeal for home missions.[8]

In 1817, the constitution of the Triennial Convention was changed to authorize the Board to "Appropriate a portion of their funds to domestic missionary purposes, in such parts of this country where the seed of the Word may be advantageously cast, and which mission societies, on a small scale do not effectively reach." The first missionaries to be sent out under this provision were John Mason Peck and James E. Welch. In sending these evangelists westward, the Board expressed the conviction that, "the western as well as the eastern regions are given to the Son of God for an inheritance, and that his gospel will triumph amid the settlers of the Mississippi and the sublimer Missouri, and extend to the red inhabitants of the wilderness."[9]

During the early decades of the century the Presbyterians cooperated with the Congregationalists in Home and Foreign Missions. The Methodists began a work in Ceylon in 1813 when Bishop Coke and six other men went from

8. *Ibid.*, pp. 385, 396.
9. *Ibid.*, p. 397.

America under the auspices of the British Wesleyan Connection. "The Missionary and Bible Society of the Methodist Episcopal Church in America" was organized in New York in 1819[10] and another Methodist Missionary Society appeared in the Philadelphia Conference the same year. Methodist literature came into being and played an important role in evangelism at this period. As early as 1808, Bishop Asbury proposed that one thousand dollars be appropriated by the Methodist Book Concern to publish religious tracts for free distribution. In 1817 a Tract Society was organized in New York by Methodist women.[11] The following year "The Methodist Magazine" was established and made permanent. It had been published previously for one year (1789) but had failed for lack of financial support. In 1826 the first issue of "The Christian Advocate and Journal" made its appearance in New York. It was published by the Methodist Book Concern.

Thus during the first four decades of the nineteenth century there appeared many organizations for home and foreign missions on the American scene. This movement was stimulated and inspired in part by the modern foreign mission movement in Europe. This rising tide of evangelistic passion and missionary zeal produced a vast amount of religious literature which was used of the Holy Spirit to promote missions and evangelism.

A tidal wave of evangelism came to the eastern seaboard and flowed to the frontier settlements of the "new west" about ten years before the coming of the missionary organizations and the numerous religious journals and other literature. This season of revival came to the Congregational churches in Connecticut in 1791 and in the Presbyterian churches along the eastern seaboard in 1792. It swept the colleges, beginning at Yale in 1802 and turned back the tide of French Deism. Through it, the Holy Spirit redeemed the frontier and raised the low moral standards of the rapidly increasing population of the remote settlements.

10. Buckley, J. M., *A History of Methodists in The United States*. Chas. Scribner's Sons. N. Y. 1902. p. 342.
11. *Ibid.*, p. 352.

The major part of the evangelizing of the east was done by local churches and pastors whose fame did not extend far beyond their local parishes. These churches and pastors projected the movement into the frontier regions through the migration to the west. Many pastors went with their flocks and maintained regular worship and preaching. Much of the evangelizing, however, was done by ministers who were sent out by the local missionary societies which were numerous in all of the older states.

Before the outbreak of the American Revolution, the Congregationalists of Connecticut made plans to send missionaries into the frontier settlements of Vermont, the first territory to the west. Some money was raised for this purpose but the movement was hindered temporarily by the war. It was not revived until 1793, after two years of the vital local revivals which came to the Congregational churches of that State. In 1793 the General Association of Connecticut asked four pastors to become traveling evangelists in Vermont for a period of four months each. They were to receive salaries of four dollars and a half per week and allowance of four dollars per week to supply their pulpits in their absence. Further expansion westward was hindered for a time by an agreement with the Presbyterians.

The promotion of the home missions enterprise by the Presbyterian Church was transferred to the Board of Home Missions in 1816. Presbyterian churches grew in membership from 72,096 in 1820 to 173,326 in 1830. The most rapid growth of this decade was on the frontier in New York and Ohio where their faithful missionaries preached the gospel in the most remote settlements. Thompson describes the work of these men as follows:

"All this cost heroic toil on the part of the devoted men, who generally gave up the comforts of life in the older states, that they might save the newer for Christ and His Church. They rode on long circuits through the pathless forests or over unbroken prairies where the bending of the stalks of grass showed the 'trail.' They slept at night under a tree, or beside a fire kept alight to scare off beasts of prey; or they shared the rude shelter and rough fare of the settlers. If they found homes for their families it was in rude shanties of two rooms, where they eked out an existence far from schools, physicians and stores, often laboring with their own hands. They met every form of resistance, from stolid indifference to avowed infidelity. They encountered drunkenness, lewdness, horse-racing, gambling and Sabbath-breaking in the newer settlements. But nothing disheartened them or broke down this faith in God and the gospel, and bit by bit they saw better influences becoming pervasive, and the order of a Christian civilization replacing the wild lawlessness of an earlier day."[12]

This description is a faithful presentation of the life and work of pioneer preachers who were sent into the "new west" by the Home Mission Societies of all the Christian denominations. A larger group of ministers who migrated to the new settlements met similar obstacles and won like victories for Christ and His Kingdom.

Home mission evangelism was promoted by the Baptists through local missionary societies. The Massachusetts Domestic Missionary Society sent missionaries into Maine, Canada, New York, Pennsylvania, Ohio, Illinois and Missouri.[13] They found conditions similar to those described in the paragraph above and won victories like those mentioned above. Joseph Cornell who toured New York and Canada under the auspices of this organization said that he travelled six hundred miles without seeing a minister of the gospel.

The Triennial Convention assumed this type of evangelism when they sent John Mason Peck and James E. Welch into the west in 1817. A separate national organization, The American Baptist Home Mission Society, came into being in 1832. It has had an honorable history down to the present time.

The evangelistic zeal and effectiveness of Methodist circuit riders has been noted in a previous chapter. They travel-

12. Thompson, R. E. *A History of The Presbyterian Churches in The United States.* Chas. Scribner's Sons. N. Y. 1902. p. 94
13. Newman, A. H. *A History of The Baptist Churches in The United States.* The Christian Literature Co. N. Y. 1894. p. 385.

ed over all the frontier regions during these decades under the direction of Bishop Asbury and his successors. They were devoted and successful evangelists. They had no home mission organization until 1819 when "The Missionary and Bible Society of the Methodist Episcopal Church in America" was organized.

The population of the United States was growing rapidly during this period but the membership of the churches grew more rapidly. In 1790 only five per cent of the population belonged to a church. The percentage increased to six and nine-tenths per cent in 1800 and to fifteen and one-half per cent in 1850.[14]

There was a vital and a mutually helpful relationship between the period of revival, which has been called The Second Awakening, and the beginnings and early growth of Home and Foreign Missions. The revivals preceded the missionary movements by a decade and provided many ministers. Thirty-six young men entered the ministry as a result of the awakening at Yale College in 1802. The missionary organizations stimulated and sustained the evangelistic passion by disseminating information about the needs of the frontier and the victories of the gospel there. They also provided permanent agencies for the promotion of evangelism. Many of these agencies are still functioning in this field. The evangelistic fires burned all the more brightly in American churches because of the world vision and passion which were created by the modern missionary movement.

The revival meeting was the predominant method in evangelism in this era. The Camp Meeting which came to the frontier because of frontier conditions continued for a half century as an effective agency for evangelism. The local revivals which came to the eastern states during the first decade of the movement became the accepted method in the older states for two or three generations.

---

14. Latourette, K. S., *A History of The Expansion of Christianity*, Harper and Brothers, N. Y. 1941. p. 177

CHAPTER XI

THE PERIOD OF DISUNITY

There were several forces operating in the young nation by 1830 which produced division. The spirit of sectionalism rather than of nationalism became predominant. The influences which produced the spirit of sectionalism were basically economic but they had very important social, moral and religious implications and relationships. The question of the tariff divided the country into political parties with more or less geographical divisions. The relationship of the various states to the federal government brought the issue of state's right to the very center of the life of the nation. The immigration from Ireland and southern Germany for economic betterment[1] brought large Catholic and Lutheran colonies to the frontier. The question of slavery was economical, social, moral and religious. It divided the nation into two distinct sections and the Christian denominations into Northern and Southern organizations. The philosophy of rugged individualism which was characteristic of all America at this time made for division and disunity.

Division occurred in America Christendom as a whole and in the older denominations. The schisms in some of the established denominations came about because of the revivals of the first three decades of the century. There was divided opinion as to the methods of the revivalists and the emotional extremes which appeared on the frontier. Further disagreement appeared because of the necessity of adapting methods of general promotion to meet the conditions in the sparsely populated areas of the west. These conditions brought about division and new denominations. These divisions both helped and hindered the evangelization of the frontier.

1. Sweet, W. W., *The Story of Religions in America.* Harper and Brothers. N. Y. 1939. p. 374.

The Cumberland Presbyterian Church was organized in 1810 by a group that withdrew from the Presbyterian Church U. S. A. that year. A General Assembly was organized in 1829 with eighteen presbyteries. This group appeared because of the failure of the General Assembly to adopt methods that would meet the needs of the frontier. The pivotal question was the educational requirements for the ministry. There was such a hunger for preaching on the frontier that Presbyterian leaders of that area ordained men who did not have the classical education required by the General Assembly. This led to trouble with the General Assembly and the withdrawal of Presbyterians from that body. The Cumberland Church used the circuit system very much as the Methodists did. They preached modified Calvinism with burning evangelistic zeal.[2] By 1861 their numbers had increased to one hundred thousand communicants.[3] It is very doubtful the General Assembly would have won the frontier settlers as rapidly as the Cumberlands did.

The Disciples appeared on the American scene at the very beginning of this era. Thomas Campbell, the father of Alexander Campbell, came to Philadelphia from Scotland in 1807. He was sent immediately to the Presbytery Chartiers in southwestern Pennsylvania (by the Anti-Burgher synod). Finding himself in disagreement with that group, he withdrew to become a free-lance evangelist.[4] He preached with ardent zeal in revivals held in barns, groves or homes as opportunity came to him. Soon his friends and followers organized themselves into "The Christian Association of Washington."

In 1810, Alexander Campbell came to America and became the leader of this group. The Christian Association became the Brush Run Church on May 4, 1811, and united with the Redstone Baptist Association in 1813.[5] The followers of the Campbells were nominally Baptist until 1830. They be-

2. *Ibid.*, p. 337.
3. Latourette, K. S., *A History of The Expansion of Christianity*, Harper and Brothers, N. Y. 1941. p. 196.
4. Sweet, W. W., *The Story of Religions in America*, Harper and Brothers. N. Y. 1939. pp. 340-41
5. *Ibid.*, pp. 342-44.

6888

came a separate denomination, the Disciples of Christ, in 1830. From the beginning the Disciples grew very rapidly.

The leader and chief exponent of the Disciples up to the Civil War was Alexander Campbell. He travelled extensively, holding the debates, and preaching in evangelistic meetings. He was brilliant, affable and energetic. In addition to his preaching and general promotion, Campbell was the founder and editor of "The Christian Baptist" which later became "The Millineal Harbinger."

The Protestant Methodist Church was organized in Baltimore in 1830 by a group of eighty-three ministers and about five thousand members who had withdrawn from the Methodist Episcopal Church. It grew rapidly for a quarter of a century but was divided by the slavery question in 1858. When the two groups reunited in 1877, they had a combined membership of 116,542.[6] The message and the evangelistic methods of the Protestant Methodist were similar to those of the Methodist Episcopal Church of this period. Even though they were few in numbers and a schism group, they were used of the Holy Spirit to win many to Christ in the period of national disunity.

The growth of the older denominations was slowed somewhat by division but it continued right up to the Civil war. After the disputes over the slavery question had divided some of these groups, they began intense evangelistic crusades. Within ten years after the division of Baptists into Northern and Southern Conventions, the Southern group had become as strong numerically as the entire denomination had been in 1844.

Much of the evangelizing of America in the period of national disunity was done by unattached and usually unpaid ministers of the gospel. All of the Christian denominations were represented by these earnest, sacrificial men of God. Dr. Kenneth Scott Latourette says: "To the efforts of these individual clergymen, without any central organization back of

6. *The Encyclopedia Americana*, Vol. XVIII, p. 725.

them, of several different denominations, and numbering many hundreds, was due much of the spread of Christianity on the frontier."[7]

The work of Jeremiah Vardeman who settled in Ralls County, Missouri, in 1830, is typical of this group of evangelistic preachers. He earned his livelihood by farming but preached with commanding eloquence and burning zeal. John Mason Peck said that Vardeman "did not wait for a Church to call him to preach, but that he sought out people wherever they were to be found and preached the gospel to them with such amazing power that Churches sprang up around him."[8] During his lifetime, Mr. Vardeman baptized more than eight thousand converts.

The traveling evangelists were much in evidence during these restless years. They represented all of the evangelical denominations and their ministry covered all of the states of the Union. They conducted camp meetings and revivals in the churches in all types of communities. These men won thousands to Christ and were instrumental in organizing hundreds of churches.

The outstanding evangelist of this period was Charles G. Finney. He was born in Warren, Connecticut, August 29, 1792, but was reared in Oneida, New York. There was practically no religious influence in his early life. Looking back over his life in later years, Mr. Finney said: "When I came to Adams to study law, I was almost as ignorant of religion as a heathen. I had been brought up mostly in the woods. I had little regard to the Sabbath, and had no definite knowledge of religious truth."[9]

It was while he was studying law at Adams, New York, that the religious experiences of this careful student began. While he was director of the choir in the local Presbyterian Church, the young law student was repelled by the extreme

7. *Ibid.*, Vol. IV, p. 484.

8. Douglass, R. S., *A History of Missouri Baptists*, Kansas City, Mo., The Western Baptist Bublishing Co., 1934, pp., 112-13.

9. Beardsley, Frank G., *Heralds of Salvation*, The American Tract Society, N. Y. 1939. p. 94.

Calvinism preached by the pastor, George W. Gale. After discussing the matter with young Finney, the pastor decided that he was case-hardened and advised that it was not worthwhile to pray for him. Many references to the Mosaic Institutes in his law books led Finney to purchase a Bible for personal study. He examined it with the same careful logic that characterized all his studying and came to the conclusion that it was the Word of God. This led him to the conviction that he was a sinner and was personally accountable to God. After a period of distress, he had a vital conversion experience in a secluded woodland near the town. He was twenty-seven years of age when he was converted.

The evening following his conversion experience there was a meeting in the Presbyterian Church. Mr. Finney gave a testimony which was used of the Holy Spirit to start a revival in that community which was destined to spread over all the eastern states. It was the beginning of his remarkable career as a traveling evangelist. For more than thirty years he was a flaming evangel, preaching in all the principal cities and towns of the eastern seaboard and winning thousands of people to Christ. Both his message and his methods were criticized but this criticism seemed to serve as good publicity. His modified Calvinism was attacked by some of the leaders of the churches and many people objected to the emotional demonstrations which sometimes appeared in his meetings.

Mr. Finney's contributions to vital evangelism as an educator and an author were quite as great as his contributions through his extensive preaching ministry. He became professor of Theology in Oberlin College in 1835 and President of that institution in 1852. In this relationship he influenced many young ministers as well as laymen in the churches. His book, "Lectures on Revivals", appeared in 1835 and a new edition was published in 1868. In 1936 he published "Lectures to Professing Christians" and in 1839 his "Sermons on Important Subjects" came from the press. His Lectures on "Systematic Theology" were published in 1847 and his final volumes, his "Autobiography" and "Sermons on Gospel Themes" appeared in

1876.[10] In these books, Mr. Finney served the cause of vital evangelism in his own and in succeeding generations. His preaching ministry, however, was confined largely to the states of the Atlantic seaboard.

The vital contribution of John Mason Peck to the evangelization of the frontier was made during this period. His career reveals the evangelistic methods of a large group of ministers who worked with him and under his direction. It also shows a vital relationship between the evangelization of the United States at this time and the modern missionary movement which began with the sending of William Carey to India by British Baptists.

In June, 1815, Mr. Peck, a young Baptist pastor, heard an address by Luther Rice at Poughkeepsie, New York. Mr. Rice was touring the United States in an effort to enlist the Baptists in the support of Adoniram Judson and his wife in Burma. This message from a missionary fresh from the foreign field stirred the soul of young Peck with a burning zeal for the benighted people of India. Along with this missionary compassion for the peoples of other lands came a like concern for the destitute sections on the American frontier. Even before his meeting with Luther Rice, Mr. Peck had been aroused concerning the needs of India through "The Baptist Missionary Magazine." He made the following entry in his personal diary on June 25, 1813:

"Received the last number of the Baptist Missionary Magazine. The missionary accounts from India are very interesting. How many thousands of the poor benighted heathen there are who worship the idol of the Juggernaut and adore the river Ganges, but are ignorant of the way of salvation through Jesus Christ! How can Christians in this land of high privileges sit easy and unconcerned, without contributing out of their abundance to the spread of the gospel in distant pagan lands where it never yet has shone. A large part of the American continent enveloped in darkness. Yes, under the immediate Government of the United States, there is an

10. *The Encyclopedia Americana*, Vol. XI, p. 227.

abundant field for missionary labor. How I should rejoice if Providence would open a door for my usefulness and labors in this way!"[11] Providence did open a door for Mr. Peck's life work in the new west. He was sent to the little town of Saint Louis, Missouri, by the Triennial Convention in 1817. His work on the frontier was largely responsible for the organization of the American Baptist Home Mission Society in 1832. He traveled over all of the newer states as a missionary statesman and evangelist from 1817 until his death in 1858.[12]

Mr. Peck was not primarily a revivalist but there were many conversions under his ministry. His chief contributions to the evangelization of the rapidly expanding frontier were made because of his missionary statesmanship. He preached in many revivals and made long journeys into remote regions for occasional preaching. The public proclamation of the evangel was given first place in his life's work but he used other agencies to establish a vital and self-sustaining Christianity in the heart of America. He organized many local Bible Societies which cooperated with the older societies in the east in the distribution of Bibles and tracts. He believed in the Sunday school as an effective evangelizing agency, giving much of his time and energy to the organization and promotion of Sunday schools and Sunday school associations. Although he was not highly educated himself, Mr. Peck exerted a potent influence upon public school education in the new west. He was also the founder of Alton Seminary which became Alton College later and is now Shurtleff College. His wisdom in dealing with frontier conditions is revealed by the fact that he developed and utilized a circuit system for preachers under his direction. His paper, "The Western Pioneer", was instrumental in spreading the gospel in the west as well as in eliciting support for the Home Missions Movement in the older churches of the East. Finally, this pioneer missionary statesman and evangelist was influential in organizing many Baptist churches, associations and State conventions

11. DeBlois, A. K., *John Mason Peck, New York*, The Baptist Home Mission Society, 1917.
12. *Ibid.*, p. 107.

which are still useful in winning men to Christ and establishing His Kingdom.

Mr. Peck made important lasting contributions to the evangelization of America and the world. His own and future generations have been blessed by his ministry in the restless decades just prior to the Civil War. He influenced home and foreign missions, Christian education and journalism.

Mr. Peck had some misgivings about the methods of the Camp Meeting revivalists but his attitude toward them was tolerant. Having attended a Camp Meeting in Missouri, he wrote:

"At evening of the last day I heard a young Cumberland Presbyterian attempt to preach from I Peter 1, 8. He was a young hand and made out but poorly. A Mr. Chamberlain, a Methodist, gave an exhortation, in which he began by lamenting the want of effort on the part of the people declaring that he had no faith to exhort; he reproved the people for sloth and neglect, but soon fell into a strain of the most passionate, powerful appeals to the hopes and fears of all around him. The Methodists were alternately assailed and discouraged, till he wound up by proposing to all who ever did pray, or ever would pray, to engage ten minutes by the watch as the last alternative. Upon this the members and others rushed forward to the stand, and all commenced as if with one voice. Soon a black woman and others commenced shouting. Two or three appeared in agony for mercy. The preachers would exhort them to have a little more faith, 'to struggle a few minutes longer, and God, Christ and heaven are yours!' They would constantly make appeals to those engaged to prevent the fervor and zeal from expiring. I left them about nine o'clock still engaged and I could hear them shouting at a great distance.

"All this great excitement and effect, as far as visible, might have been produced without the agency of God, and might be and seemed to be only the effect of human causes. While from the fruits occasionally manifested, I have no doubt that genuine convictions and saving conversions do some times follow such confused and disorderly meetings, yet it must be confessed that most of these cases prove false—worse than worthless.

"The method of talking to and exhorting the persons apparently under conviction is highly improper and injudicious. The whole object of the preachers and leaders appears to be to get them relieved from distress, quite irrespective of the character of the relief. Hence, were it not for the necessity of such meetings, in a thinly populated country, and the fact that God sometimes blesses very imperfect means, I would disapprove of them wholly. As they are congenial to the habits of the people, and may do some good, reaching those not otherwise accessable, they may be tolerated, and as far as practicable regulated."[13]

Peter Cartwright who was a Methodist circuit rider and presiding elder on the frontier for more than a half century made a notable contribution to the evangelism of this era. He was born in Virginia in 1785 but was reared in the wilds of Kentucky. Converted at the age of sixteen, he became an "exhorter" immediately and was a circuit rider at the age of eighteen. Mr. Cartwright was a chosen vessel of the Lord to witness and to win on the frontier. Dr. Kenneth Scott Latourette describes him as follows:

"Muscular, fearless, prepared to subdue in physical encounter any who attacked him, quick of wit and with the frontiersman's rough humor, disdaining and distrusting an educated ministry, with a hot indignation against wickedness and a consuming passion to win those about him to his faith, he was a striking and a famous figure."[14]

The strength of Mr. Cartwright's personality and his influence over the people of Illinois are revealed by the fact that he defeated Abraham Lincoln in an election for congressman in 1846.[15] He served in the Illinois legislature and was a leader in the anti-slavery movement.

13. *Ibid.*, p. 54-5.
14. Latourette, K. S. *A History of The Expansion of Christianity.* Harper and Brothers. N. Y. 1941. Vol. IV. p, 189,
15. *The Encyclopedia Americana,* Vol. V. p. 687.

This colorful preacher, evangelist, and reformer moved from Kentucky to Illinois in 1824, where he lived and labored until his death in 1872. During his lifetime he baptized some eight thousand children and four thousand adults. As a presiding elder, he influenced and directed many pastors, circuit riders, local preachers and class leaders. Through these devout and earnest men, he made a vastly important contribution to the evangelization of the westward moving frontier.

Mr. Cartwright has been called "The Camp Meeting Evangelist." He preached in many such meetings personally and was in hearty sympathy with the methods of the camp meeting revivalist. He felt that all of the emotional demonstrations were produced by the Holy Spirit. In regard to the "jerks" we venture to repeat in part of a quotation give from him above:

"No matter whether they were saints or sinners, they would be taken under a warm song or sermon, and seized with a convulsive jerking all over, which they could not by any possibility avoid, and the more they resisted the more they jerked. If they would not strive against it and pray in good earnest, the jerking would usually abate. I have seen more than five hundred persons jerking at one time in my large congregation. Most usually persons taken with the jerks, to obtain relief, as they said, would rise up and dance. Some would run, but could not get away. Some would resist; on such the jerks were generally severe.

"To see those proud young gentlemen and ladies, dressed in their silks, jewelry, and prunella, from top to toe, take the jerks, would often excite my risibilities. The first jerk or so, you would see their fine bonnets, caps and combs fly; and so sudden would be the jerking of the head that their long loose hair would crack almost as loud as a wagoner's whip."

He felt that these demonstrations were "a judgment sent from God, first, to bring sinners to repentance; and secondly, to show professors that God could work with or without means, and that he could work over and above means, and do whatsoever seemeth him good, to the glory of his grace and the salvation of the world."[16]

16. Beardsley, *Heralds of Salvation*, pp. 86-7.

The local revival became the prevailing method in evangelism in the eastern states from 1790 to the Civil War. Meetings of this type were conducted by local churches and pastors whose names are unknown to history but they were a potent factor in the evangelization of the older communities of our nation.

The one outstanding evangelist of this period was Charles G. Finney to whom reference has been made above. He never gave himself to a settled pastorate but he preached in many local revivals with pastors along the Atlantic seaboard. In 1829, Mr. Finney inaugurated a new type of evangelistic method. Being invited to New York by Mr. Anson G. Phelps, a philanthropist, he was given an unusual opportunity for evangelism. Mr. Phelps rented a church building and later bought one for Mr. Finney's use. Here the great evangelist preached daily for many months to large audiences and there were hundreds of conversions. Many invitations to other communites convinced him that he should leave this type of work and become a traveling evangelist again. After this period Mr. Finney visited most of the principal towns and cities of the eastern states.

The Camp Meeting continued to be the chief method in the evangelization of the West. It began to wane in its influence by the outbreak of the Civil War because of the development of the country. The frontier became a settled society with churches, schools and normal community life. These conditions made the Camp Meeting unnecessary but it was succeeded by the local revival type. The local revival still prevails in the section which had been served effectively by the camp meeting for the first four or five decades of the nineteenth century.

The Sunday School was discovered to be an effective evangelistic agency during the period of national disunity. John Mason Peck was instructed by the Home Mission Society to establish churches in the frontier communities but he spent much of his time and energy establishing Sunday schools. The results have revealed the wisdom of his plan. The American Sunday School Union also sent missionaries into the west to establish Sunday schools, many of which grew to be churches.

The distribution of the Holy Scriptures and other evangelical literature also appeared as an evangelistic method during this era. John Mason Peck organized many local Bible societies which cooperated with the established societies in the east in the distribution of Bibles. The American Tract Society sent John Vassar into Illinois in 1850 as a colporteur. Mr. Vassar sold Bibles, religious books and gave away tracts in a house-to-house ministry. His master passion, however, was to win people to Christ in these personal contacts. He witnessed many conversions in the homes and revivals usually followed his visits to the communities of the new West.[17] In 1851 Mr. Vassar returned to the east where he served the Tract Society for another year. He was employed later by the Dutchess Baptist Association in New York to do the same type of work. He was the first and the fore-runner of a noble group of colporteur evangelists.

---

17. Beardsley, Frank G., *Heralds of Salvation*, The American Tract Society, N. Y. 1939, pp. 124-25.

CHAPTER XII

SOME CONTRIBUTIONS OF EVANGELISM TO NATIONAL LIFE

The evangelism of the Colonial period was used of the Holy Spirit to make invaluable and permanent contributions to the culture of America. The rising tide of vital religion during the era of national beginnings also left a residue of permanent good which is still bearing fruit in the life of the nation.

During the seven decades preceding the Civil war there were many thousands of genuine conversions in all sections of the country and from all strata of society. The common people heard the Word gladly in the local revivals of the east as well as in the famous camp meetings in the frontier regions. The population of the young nation was growing very rapidly but church membership rolls grew even more rapidly. In 1790, only 5% of the people of our country were members of the churches. Seventy years later 22.7% of the population were church members. There had been a steady gain in church membership over the entire period as follows: 5% were church members in 1790, 6.9% in 1800, 8.6% in 1810, 11.2% in 1820, 13.3% in 1830, 14.4% in 1840, 15.5% in 1850 and 22.7% in 1860.[1] These many thousands of twice-born men and women were the salt of the earth in the life of our nation in its beginnings.

The wide-spread infidelity which followed the War for Independence was driven from the American scene by the vital evangelism of this era. French Deism was so firmly established in the American mind that many people despaired for Christianity. College students were sure that it was a dead issue, that the Bible was outmoded, and that the "Age of Reason" had finally come to the world. It was vital evangelism under the leadership of Timothy Dwight of Yale that sounded the

1. *Weber's Yearbook of American Churches*, 1933 edition, p. 299.

death knell of this philosophy. The revival spread from Yale to other centers of learning with similar results. The camp meetings on the frontier and the local revivals along the eastern seaboard were effective answers to Deism among the rank and file of the population. The rout of Deism was a notable contribution to the life of the nation in its early years.

Infidelity was accompanied by gross immorality after the nation had gained its independence. It threatened the very life of the infant nation. It was in evidence in college circles, in the settled communities of the east, and in the scattered settlements of the frontier. Drinking, gambling, obscenity, and dishonesty were rampant on college campuses. In the "new "west" there were drinking, gambling, Sabbath desecration, feuds which often led to murder, and infidelity to the marriage vows. These sins of the frontier were almost entirely swept from American life during the era of national beginnings. They vanished from the scene whenever the revival appeared.

Public education was stimulated and expanded by this tide of vital religion. The new evaluation of the individual personality which always comes with the spread of the gospel led people to see the need for universal public education. John Mason Peck, the pioneer Baptist Missionary to the new west, spent much time and energy in promoting public schools. Peter Cartwright, the colorful Methodist circuit-rider and camp meeting evangelist, was also a friend of the public school. Other leaders in the evangelism of this era also gave support to the rise of public education, especially on the frontier.

During the first sixty years of the nineteenth century many new Christian colleges arose in our country. Schools of all grades were established in all sections of the country and by all the major Protestant denominations. As exemplifying this extension of schools, let us look at one denomination whose efforts were at the same time being impeded by other troubles: the Methodists. The Methodists were agitated over the question of slavery more than any other group, yet they made a remarkable record in establishing schools during this era. Wesleyan Seminary was established in New York in 1819 and Augusta College came into being in 1822. Maine Wesleyan Seminary was founded in 1827. Wesleyan and Wilberforce Universities were both chartered in 1831. Randolph Macon was established in 1832 and three other schools—Vermont Seminary and Female College. Allegheny College, and McKendree College—were founded in 1834. Indiana Asbury University obtained a charter in 1836 and Emory College in 1837. Williamette University, Baldwin University, and Mount Union College were founded in 1844. Northwestern University appeared in 1851, Iowa Wesleyan in 1854, and Garrett Biblical Institute in 1855. Many of these institutions, as well as those established by other denominations, are now making rich contributions to American culture. They were the issue of the evangelistic impulse.

Religious journalism was produced by the evangelism of the period of national beginnings. The names and dates of the founding of many religious and missionary journals appear in the story of the beginning of Home Missions in chapter three. Their numbers and influence continued to grow up until the Civil War broke out. Publication societies also were formed to distribute Bibles, religious books and tracts. This religious journalism is making a vastly important contribution to the advancement of the Kingdom of God all over the world. It has proved and is proving to be a helpful leaven in the life of our nation. These streams of spiritual life found their beginnings in the periods of revival. They were called into being by the evangelistic impulse, and to promote the revival by disseminating information. They also carried news of the world-wide modern foreign missions movement which was then in its infancy.

The missionary organizations which were born during this era of revival are still making vast contributions to the life of America and of the entire world. Missionary conventions and mission boards appeared in the life of our nation soon after the local revivals of the 1790's. They were local at first but have grown into large national and sectional organizations which elicit the support of millions of Christians. Under the leadership of these organizations, the gospel has reached every section of America and has been sent to many foreign countries. They have developed a Christian statesmanship which holds promise of a better world tomorrow. Modern foreign missions have received and are receiving both men and money as a result of this period of revival.

Several new Protestant denominations came to the American scene during this period of spiritual awakening to enrich the culture of the nation. The Cumberland Presbyterians withdrew from the General Assembly and became a separate denomination because of the revival. The Disciples appeared as a union movement seeking to unite all Protestants. Presbyterians, Methodist and Baptists were divided into Northern and Southern groups. The formation of these new denominational groups was followed by a decade of unprecedented growth in church membership. In 1850, the ratio of church members to the total population was 15.5%, but it had increased to 22.7% in 1860.

Several factors contributed to this rapid growth. New movements are begun with an enthusiasm which is contagious. The element of competition also spurred the new groups to activity. The formation of new missionary and evangelistic organizations (such as the Home Mission Board of the Southern Baptist Convention) to promote evangelism accelerated the growth in church membership. The cumulative results of six decades of successful evangelism appeared just before the nation was engulfed in the holocaust of war.

Some new techniques in evangelism were developed during the period of national beginnings. The camp meeting appeared on the frontier, played a vital role in the Christianization of the young nation and began to wane in its influence by the end of this era. Denominational promotion of evangelism through national or sectional organizations had its beginnings in the early years of this period, but the organization of the Southern groups came late in the period. This method is still producing good results. The use of the Sunday school as an evangelizing agency was begun on the frontier. It has been developed and is now a vital factor in evangelism all over the nation. The colporteur evangelist came to the frontier and spread Christianity through a house-to-house ministry. The local revival under pastoral leadership was used of the Holy Spirit to inaugurate this era of spiritual conquest. It has continued to the present time as an effective evangelizing agency in many sections of the country.

A more pronounced denominational consciousness and loyalty came to characterize American Christendom during this period. It was a result of certain developments in evangelism. The new denominational groups felt that they needed to justify their existence on doctrinal grounds. The preaching of their distinctive doctrines challenged the older groups to defend their tenets. They also attacked the doctrinal statements of the younger groups. Denominational loyalty and solidarity were promoted also by the missionary organizations. These appealed to their constituency for support, thus creating a more pronounced denominational consciousness. The Bible and Publication Societies which were born in this era of vital and effective evangelism were also denominational. They were supported by their constituencies and, in turn, they promulgated the distinctive doctrines and gave news of the accomplishments of their own groups. This accelerated the growth of the denominational spirit. The Christian schools which were launched in this era sought and obtained the support of their church groups, teaching their distinctive tenets. The majority of the pupils in such schools came from the homes of the supporting churches and returned to their home communities with a deepened loyalty to the denomination. Thus there came to American Christendom a greater degree of denominational loyalty and conviction than it had ever known before.

The evangelistic fires which burned in all sections of the country during the period of national beginnings helped to establish evangelical Christianity more firmly in the life of the nation. Evangelical Christians became more numerous. Their organizations developed rapidly. They established educational institutions and benevolent enterprises which have been of inestimable value. The religious literature which they produced has influenced the nation toward righteousness. The foreign mission boards which came into being in this era have helped to create international and interracial understanding and good will, thus laying the foundations for world peace. The preaching of distinctive doctrine and the promotion of the missionary, educational, and benevolent work of the various groups produced a militant Christianity. It is more aggressive and able to deal with the problems of the post-war world because it has produced a type of Christian statemanship with a world-wide outlook. An American leader said recently that foreign missions have produced the largest reservoir of international good will that is in the world today. The foreign missions enterprise among American Christians was born in this era of revivals.

DIVISION THREE

THE PERIOD OF NATIONAL MATURITY—1860-1944

CHAPTER XIII

EVANGELISM IN WAR AND RECONSTRUCTION

The War between the States brought the sharpest decline in the evangelistic work of the churches ever experienced by American Christendom. After a steady gain in church membership from five per cent of the total population in 1790 to twenty-two and seven-tenths per cent in 1860, there was a recession to seventeen and five-tenths per cent in 1870. Every war in our country's history had checked and turned back the evangelistic advance, but this decade set a new record for waning efforts and decline in tangible results.

The spirit of war is counter to the spirit which sends a Christian out to share his blessings with his unsaved neighbor and which constrains Christians to form and promote organizations for the same purpose. The spirit of suspicion and animosity was rife all over the United States during the four years of war and the period of reconstruction which followed. The public mind was also absorbed by the affairs of that unfortunate strife. Therefore the spirit of evangelism waned.

The war brought a serious disruption of the church life which hindered the work of our Lord in general and evangelism in particular. A Methodist circuit rider began his ministry on a Virginia circuit in 1859 at a salary of one hundred dollars per year. His remuneration remained the same through 1860, but in 1861 when the war "swept the men in western Virginia counties into the armies" his income from the same churches dropped to seventeen dollars and fifty cents for the year. That was a decline of eighty-two and one-half per cent in one year in pastor's support. Their zeal and effectiveness in winning others to Christ declined proportionately.[1] During the quadrennium from 1859 to 1863 the Meth-

1. Hughes, Idwin Holt, *I Was a Minister*, Nashville, Abingdon-Cokesbury, 1943, p. 19.

odist Episcopal Church lost 59,451 members and probationers.[2]

The agitation and the animosity which appeared in most extreme forms in the border states disrupted church life and hindered evangelism more than in other areas. The experience of Dr. S. B. McPheeters, pastor of the Pine Street Presbyterian Church of Saint Louis, Missouri, in 1862 reveals the suspicion, distrust and animosity which existed. Dr. McPheeters had taken the oath of allegiance to the federal government twice. He had abstained from "political preaching and praying" and had been outspoken in defense of the policy of silence upon civil questions for some time. But in 1862 a member of the church presented a child to be christened and gave is the name of a famous Confederate soldier. The Unionists detested the Southern military leader. The pastor could not refuse to give the child the name chosen by the parents but, when he did, some members of the church appealed to the Provost-Marshal General of the Department of Missouri and secured the banishment of the pastor and his wife from that military district. He was banished from his pulpit for more than a year for christening the baby and for praying "for kings and those in authority" and not specifically for President Lincoln. Dr. McPheeters appealed his case to the President and Mr. Lincoln ordered that he be permitted to return to his pulpit immediately and directed that the army not interfere with the work of the churches. The military authorities, however, kept the pastor away from his people for a full year upon a legal technicality.[3]

Public resentment against some religious groups because of the agitation over slavery and the race problem hindered evangelism in many sections of the South for some years after the close of the war. The Methodist Episcopal Church, South suffered greatly from this resentment. On September 13, 1866, the Reverend Anthony Bewley was lynched in the city of Fort Worth, Texas. This Methodist minister had been falsely accused of inciting an insurrection among the Negroes.

2. Buckley, p. 516.
3. Thompson, p. 194.

He escaped from Fort Worth but was apprehended and brought back and mobbed. On Sunday, March 13, 1866, "while Bishop Janes was conducting the Arkansas Conference and was about to preach, Judge Roberts, accompanied by a mob, entered the church and notified the Bishop to leave within two hours, declaring that if the church did not cease to work . . . blood would be shed and the responsibility would be on the Bishop and the conference."[4] It is notable that it was the judge of a court of law that led the mob in this instance.

The casualties of the four years of war thinned the ranks of church members and contributed to the alarming decline. Robert Ellis Thompson, a Presbyterian historian, describes the results in that communion as follows: "The close of the war brought with it the necessity for a change in the style of the Southern church, which now took the name 'The Pres- byterian Church in the United States.' It had suffered heav- ily, as had the South, from the devastations of the war and the loss of both men and means. Churches, in some cases, had broken up never to gather again. Wounds and the dis- eases of camp and march had thinned out its membership."[5]

The economic impoverishment of the South also hindered the evangelistic advance for some time after the war. Wealthy families who had provided financial support for the churches were left in direst poverty. Their slaves had been set free, their young men had been killed in battle, their savings had been spent in the prosecution of the war and many of their plantations had been pillaged. For a time at least, they had no resources to invest in the spread of the gospel.

A social order which had been feudal in its grandeur in the South had been swept away by the war and the freeing of the slaves. A new social order had to arise out of the ashes of the old. Adjustments had to be made in the lives of both the whites and the Negroes. Many problems arose as to the church life of both groups. There were many slaves who were members of the white churches before the war. Should

4.   Buckley, p. 508f.
5. Thompson, p. 163.

the freed men remain as members of the churches along with their former masters? If they were to form churches of their own race, how could a leadership be trained for them? Were their former owners responsible for the spread of the gospel among them? There was much animated debate on these questions in the general meetings of the various denominations for ten years after the hostilities were ended. Other less appropriate questions emerged and were discussed vehemently. Even the question as to whether the Negro has a soul was seriously debated in the general meetings of some religious groups. This agitation slowed the evangelistic advance.

The greed and corruption of many politicians of reconstruction days fanned race hatred into a flame. This disturbed a society which had in it the seeds of social injustice and race discrimination. The franchise was granted to the freed men in many states and some of them were elected to offices of responsibility before they were ready for such positions. The method used by some politicians to get the Negro vote aroused the whites and brought into existence such organizations as the Ku Klux Klan. With feeling running high and agitated by all of these conditions, it was difficult to enlist Christians in the labor of love which is evangelism.

The forces described above snuffed out the fires of evangelism in many sections of the country and they burned low in the rest of the nation. These fires were not extinguished, however, even by this fratricidal strife. They burned brightest in the armies of the Confederacy.

A revival came to the Army of Northern Virginia in the fall of 1862 which continued with increasing effectiveness until the close of the war. A minister who participated in it gave the following statement of the results which reveal its growing power: "I make the following estimate of the number of men in the Army of Northern Virginia who professed faith in Christ during the four years of its existence. During the fall and winter of 1862-63, and the spring of 1863, there were at least 1500 professions. From August 1863, to the 1st. of January 1864, 5,000 found peace in believing. From January,

1864, to the opening of the Wilderness Campaign, at least 2000 more were added to this number. And from May, 1864, to April, 1865, it is a low estimate to put the number of converts at 4,000.[6] This same chaplain says that there were a total of 150,000 conversions in all of the Confederate armies during the four years of war. His estimate of the value of this revival is not confined to the number of conversions. He says:

"But figures can not, of course, give the tithe of the results of a great revival. The bringing back of backsliders, the quickening of the zeal, and faith, and general consecration of God's people, the comfort, the joy, the peace, the strength for hardships, privations, sufferings, trials temptations—these can not be counted, but are really of far more value than mere numbers of professed converts. Add to all this, the joy and gladness which these revivals carried to the 'loved ones at home' who were wont to spend sleepless nights thinking of, and praying for the soldier boy at the the front, and the reflex influence upon the churches, many of which were blessed with great revivals, directly traceable to our army work, and eternity alone will be able to estimate the glorious results of these army revivals."

These were remarkable visitations of the power of God. There were faithful men in the army through whom the Spirit of God could work. The seventy years of successful evangelism which preceded the war had produced a virile Christianity which sent many genuine witnesses for Christ into the armed forces.[7] The testimonies of these ordinary soldiers turned many of their unsaved comrades to Christ.

Many of the leaders of the Confederate forces were devout and zealous Christians. The passion of General Robert E. Lee for the souls of men is revealed in his own words as follows: "I shall be disappointed, Sir; I shall fail in the leading object that brought me here, unless these young men become real Christians; and I wish you and others of your

6. Jones, J. W., *Christ in The Camps*. B. F. Johnson and Co, Richmond, Va. 1887. p. 390
7. *Ibid.*, p. 17ff.

sacred profession to do all you can to accomplish this" and "I dread the thought of any student going away from the college without becoming a sincere Christian" and, "Our great want is a revival which shall bring these young men to Christ."[8]

These statements were made by General Lee shortly after the war when he was president of Washington College (now Washington and Lee University). His attitudes during the war, however, reveal a similar concern for the spiritual welfare of the soldiers of his command. He attended the services during the revivals among his men. A chaplain who was intimately associated with him says that, "He did quietly and unostentatiously speak a 'word in season' and exert influences potent for good in directing others into the path of heaven." His support of the chaplains and other Christian workers was sincere and enthusiastic. This was a mighty influence on promoting the revival.[9]

The famous General Thomas J. Jackson was also an ardent supporter of the revivals. He had showed an evangelistic zeal by teaching the Bible to his own slaves on Sunday afternoons for many years before the war. His Sunday school class for his Negro slaves grew into a Sunday School to which many slaves came. A short time before his death at Chancellorsville, General Jackson sent a check for fifty dollars to buy books for this Sunday school.[10] A chaplain who had never met General Jackson approached him with a request that a colporter be allowed to work among the soldiers. He gladly granted the request and asked the privilege of meeting the colporter personally. When the colporter was presented, the General gave him hearty encouragement and offered his personal assistance in distributing Bibles and religious literature, saying that he was anxious for his men to be "good soldiers of the cross."

Another reason for this remarkable revival was that Christian workers other than the chaplains were permitted

8. *Ibid.*, pp. 76-7.
9. *Ibid.*, p. 67.
10. *Ibid.*, pp. 85-7.

to work among the soldiers. The Home Mission Board of the Southern Baptist Convention had been in existence only fifteen years when war came. In that brief period, however, this board had "sent forth 750 missionaries, added 15,000 new members to the churches, built over 200 houses of worship. constituted 200 new churches and had collected and distributed about $300,000."[11] This entire force of effective evangelists turned their attention to the men in uniform and won thousands of them to Christ.

The Baptists were not alone in this crusade among the soldiers. All of the major denominations sent ministers to preach to them and an interdenominational organization was called into being by the challenge to win the men in uniform to Christ. A Presbyterian historian says:

"The armies themselves were in many cases schools of the new life to those who entered them. In that of the Confederate States there was a revival in 1863-64, which fairly outran the power of the chaplains, and volunteer workers to cope with it. In the Army of the United States the chaplains, with a few unworthy exceptions, were picked men, whose labors were fruitful of good both while the war lasted and ever since. They were aided by the labors of the Christian Commission, in which all the orthodox churches cooperated in sending preachers, nurses, supplies for well and wounded, libraries and religious literature both to the armies in action and to the winter-quarters and hospitals. The soldiers were kept in touch with home and under home influences, and were encouraged and helped to keep up correspondence and to send part of their pay home. This kind of work was begun by John Patterson, a Presbyterian of Philadelphia, by George S. Griffith of the German Reformed Church in Baltimore; and by Rev. Benj. W. Chidlow in the West. It soon crystalized into a national organization, called into existence by the National Convention of the Young Men's Christian Association."[12]

Many of the soldiers who were converted during the war identified themselves with the churches after returning to

11. Newman, p. 455.
12. Thompson, p. 161f.

their homes. Many of them became preachers and others assumed places of leadership in the life of their churches. They were a potent force in the new day for evangelism which was to come within a few years after the close of the war.

There were two notable exceptions to the tragic decline in church membership during the decade from 1860 to 1870. The Methodists suffered severe losses during the first three years of this period but their gains in the next four years were greater than their losses had been. Their losses between 1859 and 1863 were 50,951 members and probationers, but their gain from 1863 to 1867 was 222,687.[13] Southern Baptists baptised 665,035 persons between 1860 and 1874. That was a yearly average of 44,336. During the fourteen years prior to 1860 they had baptized 36,335 persons annually. They were able to report an annual increase of 8,001 Baptists in spite of war and reconstruction.[14]

The evangelistic appeals during this era were largely a call to repentance in order to prepare to die. The horrors of hell and the glories of heaven were presented with consuming zeal to the civilian population as well as to the men in uniform. These appeals naturally received a ready response in the minds of men who were about to go into battle or who were recovering from wounds in army hospitals. But a new note began to appear in the preaching of the day as well as in other public utterances. The war to free human beings from slavery focused attention upon the value of the human personality as such. This raised the question as to the God-given rights of every individual. The struggle to preserve the nation led men to think of civil government as being ordained of God, and of His right to rule over nations and individuals. These factors laid a broader foundation for the evangelistic appeal than had appeared in the Great Awakening or in the evangelism of the seven decades prior to the Civil war.

13. Buckley, p. 521.

14. Aldredge, E. P., *Southern Baptists in World Service*, Nashville, 1936, pp. 226-27.

CHAPTER XIV

THE EVANGELIZATION OF THE UNDERPRIVILEGED

The first national Holiness camp meeting in the United States was held at Vineland, New Jersey, in 1867. The purpose of the men and women who promoted this meeting was to lead believers into a state of perfect holiness.[1] One tangible result of this first post-war camp meeting was the organization of the "National Camp Meeting Association for the Promotion of Holiness" with John S. Inskip as President. Mr. Inskip and his associates felt that they should bring the camp meeting and believers' meetings back into American church life in order that Christian perfection might be realized by believers everywhere.[2] Thus an organization appeared in American Christendom which has been effective in evangelizing the socially underprivileged groups in all sections of the United States.

Some of the conditions which called this movement into being appeared in the life of the nation long before the Civil War. Others were produced by that tragic conflict. The Methodist Episcopal Church began to give less and less emphasis to the Wesleyan doctrine of perfection in the early part of the nineteenth century. In the issue of May eighth, 1835, "The Christian Advocate and Journal," expressed regret that "Christian Holiness is at present so little talked of and so little experienced in the Methodist Episcopal Church."[3] The General Conference Journal of 1840 records a statement of the Bishops that the doctrine of Christian perfection was a leading feature of early Methodism. Their anxiety over the trend away from it appears in the statement that, "It is not enough to have this doctrine in our standard." An expression of the

1. Gaddis, *Christian Perfectionism in America*, dissertation in the library of the University of Chicago, p. 443.
2. *Ibid.* p. 445
3. *The Christian Advocate and Journal*, May, 1835.

Bishops of the Methodist Episcopal Church, South in 1870 reveals the same trend in that group. They deplored the fact that the doctrine of perfect love, "a prominent theme in the discourses of our fathers" was "being overlooked and neglected."[4]

Many earnest Methodists were alarmed by the tendency to minimize the Wesleyan doctrine of perfection in their Church. They began many years before the Civil war an effort to call their people back to this fundamental teaching of John Wesley. A revival swept over the Northern States in 1857 and 1858 which gave hope to these groups but the coming of war in 1861 swept away their opportunity. A holiness literature began to appear before the war which was to be useful in promoting the holiness movement from the period of reconstruction to the present. A monthly publication, "The Guide to Holiness," appeared in 1842 under the editorial supervision of Dr. and Mrs. W. C. Palmer. This magazine claims to be "the original holiness journal of America."[5]

The war and its immediate consequences built other foundations for the holiness movement in the United States. Religious people everywhere felt a corporate conviction for sin when the war was over. They felt that something had been wrong with the religious life of the nation or the mass murder of war would not have plagued the country. Many felt that the failure of Christians to go on to perfection and of the major denominations to emphasize this doctrine was a contributing cause to the national disaster. The corrupt rule of the "Carpet Baggers" in the South and the spirit of revenge in some sections of the North emphasized the need of inward spiritual cleansing. The poverty of the South and the period of deflation which affected the rural sections of the North until about 1868 led people to seek religious consolation in a time of suffering and uncertainty.

A religious awakening began among the Methodists of the South soon after the close of the war. DuBois says, "The

4. Clark, Elmer T., *The Small Sects of America*, Nashville, The Cokesbury Press. p. 78.
5. Gaddis. *op. cit.* p. 439.

Church had now (1866) entered upon a period of phenominal spiritual activity and experience. The impoverished financial condition of the South and the disturbed state of its industries seemed to emphasize the sense of general need for spiritual enlargement. A sound of revival was heard from one border to the other. The connectional journals teemed with news of a fruitful evangelism." There were also revivals in the Methodist Episcopal Church in the North but these did not satisfy the seekers after Christian perfection. The men and women who promoted the Vineland Camp Meeting were Methodists generally. Mr. Inskip, the first president of the "Camp Meeting Association for the Promotion of Holiness", was a Methodist.

The promoters of the Camp Meeting Association did not propose to organize a separate denomination. They decried denominationalism and sought to unite all true Christians. They sought at first to influence the older denominations toward their ideas of Christian perfection but found themselves more and more unwelcome in these groups. They also sought to make their impact upon the total Christian population through "bands" and conventions for almost a quarter of a century. But the movement split into many sects after the first effort at unification. In a period of fourteen years (1893-1907) at least twenty-five separate Holiness denominations came into being. The state and national associations became sects or the evangelizing agencies of these groups.[7]

Six radical Holiness groups which are still functioning have been formed since 1880 when "The Holiness Church" was organized. "The (original) Church of God" and "The Church of God" (headquarters in Cleveland, Tennessee) appeared in 1886. "The Apostolic Faith Mission" came into being in 1900, The "Assemblies of God" in 1907 and the "Assemblies of God (General Council) in 1914. Nine moderate groups which are still functioning appeared in the same period of time. "The Salvation Army" was transplanted from England in 1880. The "American Rescue Workers" and "The Volunteers of Amer-

7. Gaddis., *Op. Cit.* P. 459.

ıca" are American groups which have withdrawn from the
Salvation Army. They maintain the beliefs and practices of
the parent organization. "The Church of God (Anderson,
Indiana)" appeared in 1880, "The Christian Missionary Alliance" in 1881, "The Peniel Mission" in 1886 and the "Men-
nonite Brethren in Christ" the same year. "The Church of
the Nazarene" came in 1894 and "The Pilgrim Holiness
Church" in 1897. Other smaller sects have appeared and some
are functioning at the present time but these have made the
main contribution of the national Holiness movement to the
total evangelistic accomplishment of American Christendom.

The theology of the Holiness groups is chiefly Arminian.
They are predominantly fundamental and pre-millinarian in
their views. Practically all of them expect the immediate second
coming of Christ. The chief emphasis in their preaching is upon heaven as the future abode of the righteous and
eternal punishment as the doom of the wicked. Their religion
would lose most of its vitality for them if the hope of heaven
were taken from them. In their emphasis upon emotional
experiences and "other-worldiness" some of the more radical
groups have become antinomian, disregarding moral standards.

The growth of these groups has been very rapid. Statistics are available upon twenty-three sects covering the decade
from 1916 to 1926. During this ten year period the growth
of the total church membership in the United States was very
small and the total increase in the number of churches was
smaller but these Holiness groups showed an increase of fifty
per cent, in membership and in units of organization.[8]

The methods used by these zealous groups in their evangelistic undertakings are the camp-meeting, the revival meeting and believers' meetings. The first function of the camp-
meeting, however, is to lead believers into an experience of
complete sanctification. The "believers" meetings have the
same motive. They are successors to the "class meetings"
of early Methodism. The revival has the two-fold motive of
winning converts and leading believers into complete freedom

8. *Ibid.* p. 536.

from sin. Both the camp-meeting and the "believers' meetings" are uesd to win people for Christ but this motive is secondary. The Holiness people feel that if sinners see believers enter into a state of perfect holiness they will be convicted of sin and will seek salvation at the mourner's bench.

Some of the moderate groups like the Salvation Army appeal to their clientele through social service. The ministry of these groups is limited to the slum sections of the cities for the most part. The famous Salvation Army program expressed in the three s's, "Soap, soup and salvation" has found a ready response among the submerged ten per cent of the people of American cities. The Volunteers of America, The American Rescue Workers and some others have adopted this method.

The national Holiness movement has made worthwhile contributions to the total evangelistic program of American Christendom. It came into the American scene during the period of reconstruction as a non-denominational movement, has broken up into many sects but has been used of the Holy Spirit to make a vital contribution to evangelism. They have helped to maintain the evangelical insistence upon a vital personal religious experience. Their conservatism in theology has been a constant challenge to liberalism and a protest against any departure from the traditional theology. Their zeal and growth have challenged the older and larger denominations. As late as 1894 the Methodist Episcopal Church made overtures to some of these groups in an effort to retain them in that Church. Even though they have consistently drawn many of their members from the ranks of the older denominations, these sects have been successful in winning the submerged groups to Christ. These groups were and are being neglected by the wealthier and more cultured churches. Some of these sects minister to the lower stratum of society by virtue of the social and economic conditions which helped to produce them but The Salvation Army and its American descendants serve these groups by deliberate choice.

Other successful efforts to evangelize the socially underprivileged in the cities of America are being made by Rescue

Missions. The Bowery Mission of New York with its program of "lifting drifting men" and the Pacific Garden Mission of Chicago are noteworthy examples. The churches of other cities approach the submerged ten per cent through "Union Gospel Missions" supported by churches of the larger evangelical denominations. Their program of preaching and social rehabilitation have been used of the Holy Spirit to bring many to Christ.

Most of the major denominations have a department of city missions which ministers to the socially underprivileged but they do not confine their efforts to this group. The Good Will Industries of the Methodist Episcopal Church is an effective method of winning to Christ and of social rehabilitation at present. Other city mission work of the major denominations reaches this group also as a part of their work.

CHAPTER XV

YOUTH MOVEMENTS IN EVANGELISM

The rise of modern cities in England and in the United States brought into being the Young Men's Christian Association which was the pioneer youth movement for world evangelization. The first Young Men's Christian Association was organized in London in 1841 by George Williams.[1] Mr. Williams had migrated to London from a rural community and had found employment in a dry goods store. This firm employed a total of eighty young men most of whom came from rural communities. These young men who were away from home and their home churches for the first time felt a deep need of Christian fellowship, Bible study and worship.

Mr. Williams led in the organization of the first Young Men's Christian Association to minister to the spiritual and mental needs of young men of his own occupation. Membership was also limited to young men who showed clear evidence of a genuine conversion experience. It was a democratic movement governed by a small board selected by the members.

The movement found a ready response in the hearts of young men of all occupations. Bible classes and prayer meetings were soon organized in other business houses of London. These meetings brought together other groups of young men who professed conversion and who yearned for fellowship with others of their kind. Such young men were naturally interested in sharing their Christian experience with others. This concern for others was deepened by their fellowship, Bible study and prayer.

Four years after the initial organization was formed the Young Men's Christian Associations of London employed a

1. *The Encyclopedia Americana*, Vol. 29. p. 652.

missionary to young men. They also promoted personal evangelism, Bible classes for young men and evangelistic meetings. The zeal of these groups, their evangelistic methods and their approach to men of their own age and condition produced a rapid growth. Within ten years there were twenty-four associations in the British Isles with twenty-seven hundred members.

It was the London movement that aroused interest in the United States and led to the organization of the first Young Men's Christian Association in our country. Captain Thomas V. Sullivan, a Christian worker among American seamen, read a letter dated October 30, 1841, which described the work of the London association. He felt the need of a similar movement in the United States where young men were also migrating to the cities. Under his leadership an organization was formed in the Old South Meeting House in Boston on December 29, 1851. Young men who were members of evangelical churches in good standing were invited to join the movement. This organization gave more attention to the social needs of young men than did the London association. The movement was promoted so vigorously by the Boston group that twenty-six associations were organized within three years.

An international organization was formed in Paris in 1855 with representatives from the British Isles, the United States, Germany, Switzerland, France, Holland, Belgium and Italy participating. The statement of belief adopted at this convention reveals that the movement was evangelical in doctrine and evangelistic in motive. The statement follows:

"The Young Men's Christian Associations seek to unite those young men, who, regarding Jesus Christ as their God and Saviour according to the Holy Scriptures, desire to be His disciples in their doctrine and in their life, and to associate their efforts for the extension of His Kingdom among young men."[2]

The Young Men's Christian Association in New York had established noon-day prayer meetings for men before the

2. *Ibid.* p. 645.

money panic of 1857 came upon our country. The prayer
meeting movement had also reached many other cities. It
was through these meetings largely that the revivals of 1857
and 1858 swept the northern states. During this two years of
spiritual awakenings more than three hundred thousand people were won to Christ and added to the evangelical churches
of the United States.

A ministry to the soldiers of the Civil War was inaugurated during the first months of that struggle by John Patterson, a Presbyterian elder of Philadelphia, George S. Griffith of the German Reformed Church in Baltimore and Rev.
Benj. W. Childaw in the west.[3] This work so impressed
the Young Men's Christian Association of New York
that they suggested the formation of a national association
to minister to the sick and the wounded especially. Other
associations joined the New York group in urging such a
movement and the United States Christian Commission was
formed. The Commission sent more than five thousand men
and women to work among the soldiers. Young Dwight L.
Moody was the first representative of this organization to
work among the soldiers. In addition to ministering to the
sick and the wounded, keeping the soldiers in touch with home
and helping with personal problems, these representatives of
the United States Christian Commission conducted evangelistic meetings and did much personal soul winning.

Since the Civil war the Young Men's Christian Association has grown to be a great international movement. It has
enlarged the sphere of its activities and is rendering an invaluable service to young men around the world. Its work of
evangelization, however, has declined. Some evangelistic
work is still being done among young men but this has ceased
to be the central passion and purpose of the organization in
the United States.

The second great youth movement for world evangelization to appear upon the American scene was the Student Volunteer Movement for Foreign Missions. The name of this or-

3. Thompson, Robert Ellis, *A History of the Presbyterian Church in the
United States*, Chas. Scribner's Son's, N.Y. 1902. p.p. 161-162.

ganization emphasizes the fact that its primary motive was to enlist volunteers for foreign mission service and to inform and inspire pastors and laymen in this country to give support to foreign missions. It has made a vital contribution, however, to the work of evangelism in the United States.

This movement was born in a meeting of college and university students at Mount Hermon, Massachusetts, in 1886. The majority of these students had been born during or soon after the close of the Civil War. They had grown up in the era of reconstruction when many serious-minded people felt a deep conviction for sin. In the minds of many there was a sense of national apostasy and failure. The social and economic conditions which the war produced had affected the lives of all college and university students of that generation. The pendulum in evangelism was already swinging back toward greater accomplishments as is revealed by the growth in church membership. In 1870 only 17.5% of the people of the United States were church members. The ratio increased to 20.4% in 1880 and to 22.4% in 1890. The Young Men's Christian Association was functioning effectively in the field of evangelism. The great meetings conducted by Moody, Bliss and Sankey were stirring American cities and attracting much favorable attention. The modern foreign missions movement was approaching its centennial and was challenging Christian youth everywhere. Carey, Judson, Moffatt, Livingstone and other pioneer missionary heroes had lived and God had wrought mightily through them. The accomplishments of foreign missions and the heroism of pioneer missionaries were a challenge to college youth of 1886.

It was in an atmosphere of national conviction for sin produced by the horrors of war and reconstruction, evangelistic and missionary triumph around the world that the Mount Hermon meeting was held. It continued for four full weeks. There were two hundred and fifty-one college and university students in attendance. They came from eighty-nine schools in the United States and Canada and there were also students present from eight or ten foreign countries. One hundred of these students dedicated their lives to foreign mission service and The Student Volunteer Movement for Foreign Missions was born.[4]

The impact of this first meeting upon evangelism in our country is revealed in an address delivered by Dr. John R. Mott before a Student Volunteer Convention in Kansas City, Missouri, in 1914. Dr. Mott said:

"They went back to their colleges to pray and work and live. A revival swept the college, and in time the epithet 'Infidel Cornell' became 'Christian Cornell.' I think of Horace Rose, known to men of Iowa and Michigan. He was a member of the nine, of the eleven and of the track team. He went down to the college from such a Convention with his vision. That year, twenty-five men made decisions for the foreign field, four hundred men won in personal work declared their faith in Christ, and six hundred men were enrolled in Bible study and it was all because Horace Rose had caught a great vision."[5]

Dr. Mott's statement, made twenty-eight years after the Mount Hermon meeting, reveals that four hundred men had been won to Christ through the work of one student who had been influenced by the meeting. Six hundred men had also been enlisted in Bible study and twenty-five had given themselves to service on foreign soil.

The Student Volunteer Movement for Foreign Missions has stimulated evangelism in the United States by its famous slogan, "World Evangelization in this Generation." This slogan had inspired college youth to win their neighbors to Christ as well as to go out as missionaries to other lands. The vast amount of missionary literature emphasizing human need and the adequacy of Christ to meet it has inspired evangelists in the homeland to a marked degree. Many young men and women who volunteered to be foreign missionaries under the influence of this organization have not actually reached for-

4. Courier, Raymond P., *The Christian Mission in the World Today,* The Student Volunteer Movement, N. Y. 1932, pp. 193 and 111.
5. *Students and the World-Wide Expansion of Christianity,* The Student Volunteer Movement, N.Y. 1914. p. 365.

eign fields but they have been earnest witnesses for Christ at home. Others have caught the vision of world evangelization but have not offered themselves for foreign service. They have been and are now winning many to Christ in our country. A recent survey revealed that the decade from 1900 to 1910 marked the greatest evangelistic advance all over the world in the history of the Church. The Student Volunteer Movement for Foreign Missions contributed to this advance.[6]

Since the dawn of the twentieth century many efforts have been made by American Christians to minister to students in secular schools. The secularization of the public school curriculum which began about 1750 was completed by the close of the Civil War. The rapid growth of state supported schools for higher education has been a phenomenon of this period of our history. The population of the United States "a little more than tripled" between 1870 and 1930 but the college and university population increased fourteen hundred per cent. The increase in state schools was three times that in privately supported schools, most of which were denominational colleges and universities.[7]

This trend aroused the Christian denominations to provide for the spiritual nurture of their members who were students in state schools. The Presbyterians were pioneers in this field, beginning their work in 1903. The General Assembly meeting that year appointed "A special committee of five . . . to ascertain to what extent our young people are in state universities and what is being done to give them religious culture and safeguard them for the church."[8] This investigation led to the placing of University Pastors by the General Assembly. The Congregationalists, the Baptists, the Methodists and the Disciples followed in rapid succession and the University Pastor became a recognized denominational leader ministering to students on the campuses of great universities.

---

6. *Christendom*, Vol. 8, No. 4 (a current magazine) p. 534.
7. Shedd, Clarence P, *The Church Follows Its Students*, Yale University Press, New Haven, 1938. p. 7
8. *Ibid.* p. 14.

The motive of this movement to minister to students was not definitely evangelistic except in the sense that to conserve the faith and Christian testimony of college and university students is evangelistic. The stated purpose of each denomination in launching its work was to conserve the students for service in the church of their childhood.

World War I brought further development in student work but the chief motive continues to be conservation rather than conquest. The Baptist Student Union, the student movement among Southern Baptists, is distinctive in this field in that it is an inter-college movement to minister to Baptist students whether they are in state or denominational schools. This movement does have a definite evangelistic emphasis even though it may be a minor emphasis. Baptist students are led to look to their own spiritual growth. The leaders have demonstrated that maximum Christian living is the way to live satisfactorily on a college campus. They are urged to share in all of the life of the church in the vicinity of the campus as well as to participate in the religious life of the college and the denomination. Many of these Christian students conduct "Youth revivals" in the churches during the vacation period in which many people are won to Christ.

The trend in Christian Youth Movements in the United States has been away from the soul-winning phase of New Testament evangelism. The Young Men's Christian Association and The Student Volunteer Movement for Foreign Missions still seek to lead men to a personal commitment to Christ as Lord and Saviour. This has ceased to be the master-passion of these groups, however. The movements which have appeared since 1900 have sought chiefly to conserve the faith and the Christian witness of college and university students. If they accomplish this they make a contribution to evangelism by "perfecting the saints." This is an important phase of New Testament evangelism. Christian Endeavor, Baptist Young People's Union, Epworth League and Walthar League, Pilgrim Fellowship and all other Christian Youth groups make a contribution to this phase of evangelism also. All of these organizations have appeared since 1890.

CHAPTER XVI

THE GREAT ERA OF MASS EVANGELISM

Post-war America was steeped in the tradition that the mass revival meeting was the method in evangelism. From the days of the Great Awakening when Frelinghuysen, Edwards, Whitefield, Tennent and others preached to weeping throngs to the outbreak of the tragic War between the States multitudes had been turned to God by the fervent preaching of revival preachers. The local revival had been the pattern of evangelistic method in the east for seventy years and had largely supplanted the famous camp meetings of the west and south. The camp meeting had appeared on the frontier where it had been a mighty agency in evangelism. Its usefulness waned with the disappearance of the frontier and it had almost disappeared from the American scene by 1860. The local revival was the prevailing method after the settlement of the country. The colporteur evangelist had also come to the frontier to distribute Bibles and religious literature and to do personal soul-winning. His personal work however was to prepare for public meetings of the revival type. The Sunday school was emerging as an evangelizing force before the war but its chief function was to prepare for the revival meeting and to participate in it. To the mind of the average American of the post-war era, evangelism and the revival meetings were synonomous. The effectiveness of this method appears in the fact that in the seventy years prior to the Civil War the membership of the churches had increased from 5 per cent of the population to 22.7 per cent.

When the war was over and the people had reflected upon it there came to many serious minded people a conviction for sin. The distress of the post war era also led men to seek God. Under these conditions it was natural that the revival method in evangelism should come into a new day of prom-

inence and power. For such a time as this God raised up
Dwight Lyman Moody who was to be the apostle of mass
evangelism for two generations and whose ministry will likely influence many succeeding generations. It is the opinion
of an eminent Church historian now living that Moody and
Sankey have determined the revival methods of American
Christians since their day.

Mr. Moody was twenty-four years of age when the war
began. His success in evangelism through two mission Sunday schools in Chicago over a period of four years and his
experience in the Young Men's Christian Association of that
city over a period of three years had prepared him to work
and to witness for Christ among the soldiers.[1] He had given
up business to devote his life to religious work in 1860—one
year before war came.[2]

His evangelistic ministry among the soldiers was a further schooling to prepare Mr. Moody for his great career. His
first work during the war was in Camp Douglas near Chicago. In the temporary chapel erected there, he and his associates of the United States Christian Commission conducted
more than fifteen hundred meetings. An associate describes
one of these services as follows:

"They came to the altar—twenty, thirty, forty, at a time.
We closed the meeting and began inquiry work. Moody had
the platform and God used him wonderfully. 'God is here!',
Moody whispered to me."

The fact that these recruits were merely passing through
Camp Douglas and could not attend many services impelled
the evangelists to urge an immediate acceptance of Christ as
Saviour and Lord. This urgency appeared in all of Moody's
evangelistic appeals throughout his entire career. It was in
personal evangelism, however, that this ardent young Christian worker learned his most important lessons during the
war. Wounded men could not be brought together in a chapel

1. Hansen, J. W., *The Life and Works of the World's Greatest Evangelist, Dwight L. Moody,* W. B. Conkey Company, Chicago, 1900, p. 68
2. *Encyclopedia Americana,* p. 422.

to hear the word preached. They had to be dealt with individually and with many of them it was "now or never." The urgency of his appeals to such men is revealed in Mr. Moody's own words as follows:

"We were taking a large number of wounded men down the Tennessee river after the battle of Pittsburg Landing. A number of the young men of the Christian Commission were with me, and I told them that we must not let a man die on the boat that night without telling him of Christ and Heaven.

"You know the cry of a wounded man is for 'Water! Water!' As we passed along from one to another giving them water we tried to tell them of the water of life, of which if they would drink they would never die."

Mr. Moody also gave the following account of using the Scriptures in helping a wounded man. He had been invited to the cot of this young man late at night to "help him die." The young man felt that he was too great a sinner to be saved in his last moments. In helping him Mr. Moody said:

"I read from the third chapter of John, how Nicodemus came to the Master. As I read on, his eyes became riveted upon me and he seemed to drink in every syllable. When I came to the words, 'As Moses lifted up the serpent in the wilderness, even so must the Son of Man be lifted up: that whosoever believeth in Him should not perish, but have eternal life,' he stopped me and asked:

" 'Is that there?' "

" 'Yes,' I said.

" 'Well,' he said, 'I never knew that was in the Bible. Read it again.' Leaning on his elbow on the side of the cot, he brought his hands together tightly, and when I finished he exclaimed:

" 'That's good! Won't you read it again?' Slowly I repeated the passage the third time. When I finished I saw that his eyes were closed, and the troubled expression on his face had given way to a peaceful smile. His lips moved, and I bent over him to catch what he was saying, and heard in a faint whisper:

" 'As Moses lifted up—the serpent—in the wilderness,—
even so must the Son of Man be lifted up:—that whosoever—
believeth on Him—should not perish, but have eternal life.'

"He opened his eyes and said: 'That's enough, don't read
any more.' Early next morning I came to his cot, but it was
empty. The attendant in charge told me the young man had
died peacefully, and that after my visit he had rested quietly, repeating to himself, now and then the glorious proclamation: 'Whosoever believeth on Him should not perish but
have eternal life.' "

It was through hundreds of experiences like this that Mr.
Moody learned to do personal work, using the Word of God
and urging an immediate yielding of one's self to Christ as
Saviour and Lord. The effectiveness of his personal and public evangelism in the armies is revealed by a statement made
by Moody some thirty years after the close of the war. He
wrote: "For more than thirty years I have been continually
meeting men who were converted in those army meetings."[3]

After the war Mr. Moody's fame spread so far that he
was invited to make a tour of the British Isles. Here he
preached to great throngs and witnessed hundreds of conversions. Upon his return to the United States, he began
his career as a traveling evangelist in his homeland. His
first campaign was in Brooklyn in 1875. These meetings were
held in a large building called "The Rink" and located on
Clermont Avenue.[4] It had a seating capacity of five thousand.
The building was entirely too small to accommodate the
crowds. It was estimated that twenty thousand people
were turned away for lack of room during these meetings. This was a prophecy of the success of Moody and Sankey in many other American cities for the next quarter of a
century. It is estimated that Moody preached to fifty millions
of people in the United States during this period.[5]

3. Hansen, Op. Cit. p. 94.
4. Goodspeed, E. J. The Wonderful Career of Moody and Sankey, N.
   D. Thompson and Company, Saint Louis, Mo. 1877. p. 326.
5. The Encyclopedia Americana Op. Cit. p. 326.

Mr. Moody was a man "sent from God" for the day in which he lived. No other explanation of him is adequate. It is also easy to see the wisdom of God in his training and ex- perience which prepared him for his career. His attitude of utter devotion to Christ created in him a corresponding atti- tude of entire unselfishness. He received and disbursed large sums of money but not for himself. His methods in evangel- ism reflect these two attitudes as well as sound judgment.

Most of the publicity for the Moody-Sankey meetings consisted of news stories and editorials in the largest daily papers of the day. This was promoted, no doubt, by the Chris- tian groups who were sponsoring the meetings but it was still "news" for the papers. His career in the British Isles had been widely publicized in American papers before the Brooklyn meetings were held.

Mr. Moody was a genius in organization and promotion. He would secure the cooperation of practically all the churches in any city where he was to conduct meetings. In these groups he would organize prayer meetings a full year before the be- ginning of the campaign. Mr. Sankey would precede the evan- gelist and organize and train a large choir recruited from all of the churches to help with the worship in song. No detail of preparation or promotion was overlooked. It was his practical wisdom in prosecuting his work that won for Mr. Moody the confidence and the support of the most sucessful business men of America.

A new technique which Mr. Moody brought to American evangelism was the training and the direction of personal evangelists. He began this work in Chicago, but learned its value and much of the technique in the exigencies of the Civil war. His enquiry room became a regular feature of his meet- ings. Here the people whom he had taught how to use the Sword of the Spirit in dealing with individuals did effective personal work. Out of this beginning has grown a vast amount of educational material and an extensive program of training personal evangelists in many Christian denominations.

A second new technique which came to American evan- gelism with Moody and Sankey was the effective use of music in winning men for Christ. The music under the direction of Bliss and Sankey was quite as effective in turning men to God as was the preaching of the Word. Out of the work of these pioneers has developed the "gospel singer" as a full time Christian worker. They composed and published many hymns which are still in use. The appearance of the singer as a professional man has led to the establishing of schools for the training of such workers.

Mr. Moody's career also demonstrated that the plain preaching of the evangelical doctrines of the Bible will reach and redeem the common people. He was true to the great fundamentals of evangelical Christianity presenting these great truths in the vernacular of the streets. The results in both Britain and America reveal that the simple gospel is the power of God unto salvation.

Dr. J. Wilbur Chapman was used of the Holy Spirit to make an invaluable contribution to the evangelistic advance during the period of national maturity. He was successful as a pastor in growing evangelistic churches. He was also effective as a professional evangelist in great city-wide campaigns.

It is easy to see the providential preparation of Mr. Chapman for his dual role in evangelism. He was born two years before the outbreak of the Civil War. His childhood and adolescent years were the years of war and reconstruction. These difficult years stamped upon his mind that life is serious and must be built upon enduring spiritual foundations. As a young man he enrolled in Oberlin College soon after the death of President Charles G. Finney. The career of Finney, the man of prayer, helped to mold the life and thought of young Chapman. It was while he was a college student also that Mr. Chapman came into personal contact with Dwight L. Moody who was then in the morning of his great career as an American evangelist.

Mr. Moody's personal counsel as well as his challenging example helped to shape the career of J. Wilbur Chapman. He helped him to understand what genuine faith is in a personal

interview. Young Chapman went to Chicago to attend one of
Moody's meetings. Being uncertain at the time of his own salvation he went to the inquiry room for a personal conference
with Moody. He told Moody of his difficulty and was asked to
read John 5:24: "Verily, verily, I say unto you, He that heareth
my word and believeth on Him that sent me, hath everlasting life, and shall not come into condemnation; but is passed from death unto life." When he had finished reading, Mr.
Moody asked: "Do you believe that?" He replied, "Certainly
I believe it." "Are you a Christian?" inquired Moody. He replied. "Sometimes I think I am, and again I am fearful." Moody
requested that he read the verse again and then probed him
with the same questions. Upon receiving the same answers
Moody asked rather impatiently, "Whom are you doubting?"
Mr. Chapman then understood that he was questioning the
word of God. Mr. Moody asked him to read the verse again
and plied him with the same questions very tenderly and
earnestly. Chapman's answers were both in the affirmative
and he left the inquiry room with full assurance as to his own
salvation.

The influence of Moody appears in the successful pastor-
ates of Chapman. While pastor at Schuylerville, New York,
he attended a Moody meeting in Albany. He was so inspired
that he began to pray and to work for a revival in his own
church. The revival came and there were more than one hundred conversions in one year. His next pastorate was in a
very aristocratic church in Albany which did not reach the
masses of the people. Mr. Moody advised the pastor to use
gospel hymns to fill the pews. He introduced the gospel songs
of Sankey and others and, in spite of some initial opposition
was successful in filling the pews. Within the next five years
there were more than five hundred conversions.

His success in pastoral evangelism brought urgent appeals for Mr. Chapman to give all of his time to evangelistic
meetings. In a five year period he conducted simultaneous
meetings in more than fifty American cities with gratifying
results. There were seven thousand professions of conversion in one of these meetings and three thousand in another.

Mr. Chapman brought some new techniques to American evangelism. It was his custom to conduct simultaneous meetings in the churches rather than one great central meeting in a tabernacle. He perfected an organization to promote these movements as follows: a finance committee to provide funds for incidental expenses, a canvassing committee to visit every home in the city and invite people to attend the meetings, a music committee to organize choirs and provide music, an ushers committee to seat the congregations and to distribute decision cards, a publicity committee to keep the movement before the people and a devotions committee to arrange prayer meetings. This thorough organization was undergirded by the great prayer life of Chapman as well as by the praying of the multitudes of faithful Christians who shared with him in these simultaneous meetings.

A contemporary of Dr. Chapman, Dr. R. A. Torrey, was also an influential leader in American evangelism. He was prepared to be a "champion of orthodoxy" by his experiences in Yale University as a very young student. He entered Yale at the age of fifteen and was beset by doubts for three years. It was during his senior year that he was converted. He dedicated his life to the ministry and entered the Yale Divinity school the next year. Three years later he and a small group of Divinity School students attended a service in a meeting conducted by Dwight L. Moody. They went rather condescendingly to see what this uneducated layman might have to say. They were so impressed with Moody's message that they requested him to teach them how to win souls to Christ. Mr. Moody gave them some verses of Scripture to use and said, "You go at it. The best way to learn is to go at it. How to do it is to do it." This experience kindled the fires of evangelism in the soul of young Torrey and further prepared him for a career in evangelism.

In his first pastorate Dr. Torrey had further training for his life's work in the crucible of experience. He who had wrestled with doubt as an immature college student was called upon to deal with rampant infidelity in Garrettsville, Indiana, where his church was located. These early struggles prepared him for a distinct type of evangelistic preaching which always laid a solid foundation for faith. It was also during his first pastorate of four years that young Torrey read Charles G. Finney's "Autobiography" and "Lectures on Revival." The reading of these books from the pen of a great evangelist of the preceding generation so inspired the young pastor that he began to work and to pray for a revival. Here he led in a co-operative meeting which won many to Christ.

Perhaps his greatest contribution to American evangelism was made by Dr. Torrey through his connection with the Moody Bible Institute of Chicago and the Los Angeles Bible Institute of Los Angeles, California. He became superintendent of the Moody Bible Institute in 1889, the first year of its existence. Moody had established the school to train lay workers for his inquiry room. Dr. Torrey so directed the school that it was an effective agency in the famous "World's Fair Evangelistic Campaign" in Chicago in 1893. After leaving the Chicago school Dr. Torrey became dean of the Los Angeles Bible Institute in 1912. He continued in this position until 1924.

Dr. Torrey also served effectively as an evangelistic pastor and as a professional evangelist. From 1894 until he closed his work in Chicago he was pastor of the Moody Church as well as superintendent of the Moody Bible Institute. During his tenure as dean of the Los Angeles Bible Institute he served as pastor of the Church of the Open Door. He left the Los Angeles school and church in 1924 to spend two years in great evangelistic meetings in many American cities.

The evangelistic ministry of Rodney "Gypsy" Smith in the United States was just one phase of his world-wide ministry. Just as three prominent American evangelists—Moody, Chapman and Torrey—toured the British Isles and many other foreign countries, this effective British evangelist campaigned for Christ in America.

At least two American evangelists were used of the Holy Spirit in moulding the life of Gypsy Smith. Moody and Sankey visited a gypsy camp on the edge of Epping Forest in

England to conduct an evangelistic service. When they were about to leave the camp, Sankey put his hand upon the head of a gyspy boy and said, "The Lord make you a preacher, my boy." The boy was Rodney Smith who was destined to become the famous gypsy evangelist.[6] During the early years of his ministry in Britain, Mr. Smith read three books by Charles G. Finney—"Lectures on Revivals of Religion," "Lectures to Professing Christians," and "The Way of Salvation." These books by the noted evangelist of the preceding generation increased Gypsy Smith's knowledge of the Bible and his understanding of Christian experience. They also revealed to him the eternal principles of New Testament evangelism.[7]

Mr. Smith's first visit to America was in 1889.[8] Bearing letters of recommendation from prominent Christians in Britain, he presented himself at a meeting of Methodist Episcopal Ministers in New York. He was received very cordially. Two days later he visited the publication office of the "Christian Advocate" where he met a Dr. Clark who was serving as acting editor. He gave him a note to Dr. Prince who was pastor of the Norstrand Avenue Methodist Episcopal Church in Brooklyn. Dr. Prince was seeking for some one to help in special meetings at the time. After some hesitation Dr. Prince and his official board accepted the new evangelist from across the Atlantic and his first meeting in America began. The auditorium of the Norstrand Avenue Church which had a seating capacity of fifteen hundred was packed every evening of the three weeks campaign. The results were very gratifying, there being more than four hundred professions of conversion. This auspicious beginning brought invitations to other cities and led to many other visits to America. Up to this time Gypsy Smith has conducted evangelistic meetings in practically all the larger cities in the United States as well as in a few of the smaller centers.

6. Autobiography of Gypsy Smith, *op. cit.* p. 169.

7.Beardsley, Frank G. *Heralds of Salvation*, The American Tract Society, N. Y. 1939, p. 212.

8. Gypsy Smith, p. 165ff.

The Spirit of God was upon the gypsy boy who became a world-wide witness for Christ, but there are some evident reasons for his power in the character and the qualifications of the man. He was completely dedicated to Christ and His will. He was possessed of a humility which reminds one of Him who was meek and lowly in heart. Describing his first voyage to America, Mr. Smith said, "I felt as we slowly sailed away that I was venturing out on a great unknown, but though my confidence in myself was poor and weak enough, I was very sure of God." This statement also reveals a living faith in God, another secret of his power to win men. God endowed him with a musical voice which he used in presenting the Gospel in song as well as in sermon. He also had a quick, ready wit which often stood him in good stead. When he approached Dr. Prince of the Norstrand Avenue Methodist Episcopal Church, in Brooklyn he was rebuffed with these words, "Well, brother, I guess I don't want you." His quick reply was, "Well, Doctor, I think you do. I am no adventurer. I want you to read these (his letters of recommendation) before I leave you." Dr. Prince read the letters, and the evangelist was engaged for the meeting. Once while he was preaching to a large American audience a tall man leaped to the platform and said, "My friends, the Lord has given me a message to give to Gypsy Smith. I have to explain to you the Book of Revelation." Mr. Smith pushed him toward a chair, saying, "My good friend, the Lord has not told me to listen to you. So just sit right there until I am through." The sermon was not interrupted again.

Sam P. Jones, a noted Methodist evangelist, began his career as a traveling preacher in the Methodist Episcopal Church, South in 1872. He soon became known as an evangelist of marked ability in the South and was invited to preach in a meeting in the Brooklyn Tabernacle of which Dr. T. DeWitt Talmage was pastor. A subsequent meeting in Saint Louis brought invitations to all parts of the nation. Mr. Jones was a master at the use of slang and uncouth phraseology to attract attention and to impress the truth he sought to convey. In a sermon on "Intemperance" he spoke of the two major political parties as follows:

"The only side on which they claim to differ is that the Republicans have shouldered the nigger and the Democrats have straddled a barrel of whisky. There they are—the two parties! Here is the Democrat astride his barrel of whisky, and here is your Republican with a nigger on his shoulder. Party affiliation says you must swallow one or the other, or we will walk you out and consider you a traitor to the party. Let us look at the two a little bit. You ask me which I will take. I will say I was born, raised and have been a Democrat all my life, but if I have got to swallow a barrel of whisky in the Democratic party, or desert that party and swallow a nigger—I have lived all my life among millions of niggers in the south, and I say that all the niggers in the south never did me as much hurt as one gallon of whisky did once. If I have not got good hard sense, if I am going to exercise my good hard sense, then I meet you as an honest man who wants to do his duty, and I ask you, 'Will you become one if I choose the brother in black and gulp him down?' 'Oh,' you say, 'You will divide the party and it will go down.' I believe before God that the Democratic party has espoused the liquor interest and come out on the side of the whisky seller, and I want her to go down, down! and I have a text that will make her writhe in hell."[9]

Mr. Jones' lawyer father provided for him the best education offered in his day. A contemporary wrote, "He is one of the most sensational preachers in the world, yet his meetings produce intense interest and an immense harvest of converts, most of whom 'stick'."

The most colorful evangelist of this era of great mass meetings was Rev. William A. "Billy" Sunday. He began his career as a Christian worker with the Young Men's Christian Association in Chicago in March, 1891.[10] His first experience in evangelism was as an assistant to Dr. J. Wilbur Chapman, but Dr. Chapman left the field of evangelism to return to the pastorate January 1, 1896, leaving Mr. Sunday without employment. At this juncture an invitation came to

9. Sam P. Jones, p. 460.
10. Beardsley, *op. cit.* p. 194.

him to conduct an evangelistic meeting at Garner, Iowa. Having only eight sermons which Dr. Chapman had written for him, Mr. Sunday journeyed to that small mid-western town to begin his remarkable evangelistic career.

Billy Sunday brought the tabernacle type of evangelism to its highest peak of popularity.[11] In addition to his own personality and energy he developed and directed an extensive organization in promoting his meetings. The training of the large choirs and the direction of the music in Sunday campaigns was in the hands of Homer Rodeheaver from 1909 until the close of Sunday's career. The singing of familiar gospel hymns under the leadership of Mr. Rodeheaver would continue for some thirty or forty-five minutes before the sermon. Mr. Rodeheaver was adept in directing large crowds in singing and in selecting an appropriate invitation hymn at the close of the sermon. Other employees of Mr. Sunday were a business manager, a publicity director, a pianist, a Bible teacher, personal evangelists, and an athletic trainer. The function of the athletic trainer was to keep the evangelist in good physical condition. The business manager and the publicity director would visit a city where a meeting was to be held a year before the beginning of the meeting. They would arrange for the building of the tabernacle, secure the cooperation of all Christian forces possible and begin the work of publicity.

Billy Sunday's message was the gospel of the grace of God presented in his own unique and dynamic way. He was not a profound student nor an incisive thinker but he was a good actor. He would use slang and uncouth language in the early days of his meetings but his motive was to attract the crowds and create interest. His famous "acrobatic preaching" had the same purpose. As the meetings progressed his language became more chaste and his manner more serious as he urged men to be reconciled to God through the Christ who had come into the life of a professional baseball player and had made of him a great evangelist.

11. *Ibid.* p. 200.

Mr. Sunday's amazing hold upon his public, the common people of America, is revealed by a national poll taken by a popular magazine in 1913. The readers were asked, "Who is the greatest man in America?" Billy Sunday was one of two religious leaders mentioned and he was tied for eighth place by Judge Ben Lindsey and Andrew Carnegie.[12] It is said that a million persons "hit the sawdust trail" in the Sunday meetings to announce their acceptance of Christ as Saviour and Lord. One of Mr. Sunday's contemporaries and conservative biographers says, however, that perhaps two hundred and fifty or three hundred thousand of them were actually converted. A million people did likely shake the hand of the evangelist in response to his dynamic appeals but many were Christians already and some were simply swept along with the crowd. It is a notable achievement, however, that Billy Sunday, his group of employees and the millions of Christians who cooperated in his meetings, did actually win more than a quarter of a million people to Christ. An important feature of Mr. Sunday's ministry was his success in winning men and women who were leaders in the life and thought of the nation. The honorable Henry J. Allen, one time governor of Kansas and United States Senator from that state, was converted in a Sunday tabernacle revival. He served on a gospel team and was instrumental in winning to Christ Mr. William Allen White, another prominent Kansan. It is said that the gospel teams which were organized as a result of Sunday's tabernacle meetings in Kansas have won eleven thousand people to Christ.

The great mass meetings of the era from the Civil war to 1930 were used of God to turn millions to Christ in the United States and their influence reached many foreign countries. The membership of the churches of America which was 17.5% of the total population in 1870 grew steadily to 47.6% in 1930. This is a remarkable achievement in a nation whose population was increasing very rapidly. The great tabernacle meetings added many of these names to the church rolls.

---

12. Ellis, W. T. *Billy Sunday, The Man and His Message*, The John C. Winston Co. Philadelphia, Pa. 1914.

But Billy Sunday lived to see the tabernacle revival lose its potency and fade from the American scene. This fact grieved him deeply and he predicted a short time before his death in 1935 that this type of evangelism would regain its popularity and power. His latest evangelistic efforts were in ordinary revivals in the churches.

Many forces in American life have contributed to the decline of this method in evangelism. The most powerful perhaps has been the development of the moving picture industry. Before the rise and spread of the modern moving picture the masses of the American people found a certain emotional satisfaction in the great revivals. They now receive that satisfaction in much larger numbers and upon a much lower level in the theater. The tabernacle did not and could not have the artistic stage setting, the air-conditioned auditorium and the splendid sound effects that the modern movie house has. Neither could the tabernacles be as numerous and as accessible to all the people as are the theaters. The psychological study of the Christian experience which began in America about nineteen hundred has also contributed to the decline of the spectacular tabernacle type of evangelism. This study has in no way detracted from the necessity, the value and the reality of the Christian experience. It has not hurt genuine evangelism but it has revealed that the influences which produce the conversion experience usually begin to operate in the mind long before the actual experience comes. The conversion crisis may come in the enthusiasm of a mass meeting but the foundation was laid long before the coming of the evangelist. The revival, therefore, does not deserve as much credit for the results as people formerly thought. The training of laymen and women to do personal evangelistic work which began with Moody has found a large place in most of the evangelical churches of America. The colleges and the seminaries have also inspired and trained large numbers of evangelistic pastors. The leadership of these pastors and the work of these trained lay evangelists have made the churches less dependent upon the evangelist and the revival meeting for evangelistic results. The rise of liberalism in theology which has questioned the basic assumptions of the evangelical faith has also accelerated the decline of mass evangelism. Unfortunate efforts at imitation of some of the great evangelists has also made this approach to the multitudes ludicrous. The appearance of so many "Little Billy Sundays" imitating his peculiar pulpit mannerisms but not possessing his deep concern for the salvation of men has done great injury. Along with these cheap efforts at imitation came an unworthy desire to count large numbers of converts. The desire for numbers was often motivated by selfish ambition and a greed for gain. The methods employed to get men to confess Christ and to raise money have hurt evangelism and the professional evangelist deeply. The First World War with its organized and systematic generation of hatred, its destruction of human life and the most sacred human values dealt the death blow to the tabernacle revival. It continued for a few years after that tragic conflict but with ever diminishing effectiveness.

CHAPTER XVII

TRAINING FOR EVANGELISM

The training of personal soul-winners in an educational institution was begun in the Moody Bible Institute of Chicago, Illinois. This method was established in 1899 for the purpose of training men and women to deal with the inquirers in the famous inquiry rooms of the Moody tabernacle meetings.[1] The blessings of God have been upon this institution from the beginning. It began to draw students from all parts of the English speaking world early in its career and has continued to do so up to the present time. The teaching of personal evangelism has developed into the training of evangelistic pastors, missionaries, musicians and educational workers. Thousands of men and women have gone out from this institution with a passion to win men for Christ and equipped with training in effective Scriptural methods.

The major emphasis in the teaching of evangelism in the Moody Bible Institute continues to be upon the training of personal evangelists. In the catalog describing the courses offered in the school year of 1943-1944, the following statement appears:

"D. L. Moody, the founder of the Institute, was a most successful personal soul-winner of men and women and boys and girls before he entered the vocation of evangelist. Therefore, by God's grace, he planned that the Institute should be a place where both men and women students should always receive training in that form of service, and from which they might go forth on fire for Christ and the salvation of the lost.

"In the carrying out of this object, students are taught in the class room and by actual experience in assignment

---

1. Beardsley, Frank G. *Heralds of Salvation*, The American Tract Society, N. Y. 1939, p. 282ff.

work, how to approach their fellow men for Christ, and how
to use the Bible in dealing with different classes of individuals, emphasis being laid upon the memorizing of suitable
Scriptures to meet the various difficulties of inquirers.

"Students in the Pastors' Course are given special instruction in evangelism as it relates to the pastor and his
church"

Two courses are offered in the Correspondence School.
They are described as follows:

"**Evangelism**—one textbook, 80 pages, 13 lessons, 13 examinations. A concise, thorough complete, presentation of the
subject named.

"**Scripture Memorizing for Successful Soul-Winning**—
Two textbooks, 142 pages, 12 examinations. The student is
taught a system of Scripture memorizing and how to use it in
dealing with various classes of the unsaved."

Courses in personal soul-winning are required of all the
students in all the departments of the school. They meet one
hour per week during the first half of the school year. The
emphasis is upon using the Bible in meeting the needs of the
individual. Another course labeled "Evangelism" is offered
in some of the departments. The assignment work and the
report hour offer laboratory training in personal evangelism
as well as in public presentation of the evangel.

In addition to the inspiration and the training of evangelists, the Moody Bible Institute has produced an extensive literature. Books, tracts and periodicals have gone and are going out in great numbers to give inspiration and instruction
to the witnesses for Christ and to present the way of salvation to the unsaved. This evangelistic literature is being used
of the Holy Spirit to turn many to Christ.

Other schools of the Bible Institute type have appeared
in many parts of our country. They offer courses in evangelism which are contributing to the evangelistic advance.

The first American theological seminary to establish a department of evangelism was the Southwestern Baptist Theo-

logical Seminary of Fort Worth, Texas. The idea of such a department of instruction was born in the mind and heart of Dr. B. H. Carroll, founder and first President of Southwestern Seminary. His dream and deep desire became a reality in 1908 when "The Chair of Fire" was established with Dr. L. R. Scarborough as Professor of Evangelism.

Dr. Carroll was a pioneer and a prophet in his thinking of the place of evangelism in theological education. He was convinced that the office of evangelist was a New Testament office just as truly as was the work of apostles, pastors, teachers and missionaries. His understanding was that the work of the evangelist was different from the others in that his was to be an inter-church ministry. He held to the New Testament teaching that the first function of the evangelist was "the perfecting of the saints." He believed that this was to be accomplished through an inter-church ministry of preaching, teaching and challenge to larger co-operative undertakings.

The convictions of this pioneer as to the place and the function of the evangelist helped to mould his thinking as to the type of training he should receive in a theological seminary. This training offered to all students would lead to a better understanding of the function of the evangelist and a better co-ordination of his work with the work of other church and kingdom leaders. Dr. Carroll was convinced, therefore, that the courses in evangelism should meet the same scholarship requirements as other seminary courses. It has been said of the founding of the Southwestern Baptist Theological Seminary that, "A second departure, a new department, was the establishment of the chair of Evangelism, giving it full standing as a department in theological education, on a par with Homiletics, Greek, Hebrew, Systematic Theology, Church History and so on."[2]

In order to bring this great ideal into reality, Dr. Carroll suggested that the courses to be offered in evangelism should

2. Scarborough, L. R., *A Modern School of the Prophets*, Broadman *Press*, Nashville, Tennessee., 1939. p. 130.

give an exposition of the idea of the Kingdom of God in the Old and the New Testaments, a history of evangelism, a study of the propaganda methods of the major non-Christian religions, practical and scriptural methods in evangelism. He very wisely demanded that the Professor of Evangelism should be a successful evangelist as well as a student and a scholar.

Dr. Carroll felt that the Spirit of God had given him the vision of a full department in evangelsm and that He would lead to a man of God's own choosing to be the first Professor of Evangelism in an American theological seminary. He prayed for such leadership and his mind settled upon Dr. L. R. Scarborough, at that time the pastor of the First Baptist Church of Abilene, Texas.[3] The young pastor seemed to possess the necessary qualifications to develop the department. He was a graduate of Baylor and Yale Universities and had received one year of training in the Southern Baptist Theological Seminary and was succesful as an evangelistic pastor as well as a general evangelist.

The offer of the Chair of Evangelism to the young pastor plunged him into a terrific struggle to find and to follow the will of God. He loved the First Baptist Church of Abilene, Texas, with the love of a genuine undershepherd. The people loved and respected him as a man sent from God to be their shepherd. They were very generous in giving him leaves of absence to preach in evangelistic meetings throughout the country and he was in great demand for this type of evangelistic effort. Other calls besides the pastorate and the field of evangelism presented themselves to Dr. Scarborough. After two years, however, he was convinced that the call to establish a department of evangelism was the call of God. In 1908 he presented his resignation to the church he loved so much and linked his life with the Southwestern Baptist Theological Seminary and with the vitally important task of training for evangelism.

3. Dana, H. E. *Lee Rutland Scarborough, A Life of Service.* Broadman Press, Nashville, Tennessee., 1942, p. 80ff.

The contribution of this pioneer Professor of Evangelism to the Kingdom of God is incalculable but it is marvellous to contemplate. For thirty-four years he taught evangelism and developed his department. He gave the following description of this department in 1938:

"It was given as a four year course at first, but later changed to two years. It has all the years had the largest classes in the seminary, requiring the chapel, our largest hall, for its recitatons. It has sometimes reached the number of 250 in class. It has always been required of every student for one or two years. It was not meant that the class in evangelism should do all the teaching of evangelism, but it was expected that all the teachers would put into their teaching an evangelistic motive, passion and power."[4]

Hundreds of men and women whose lives have been invested in the furtherance of the gospel around the world have received inspiration and vitally important information in these classes. But the professor's influence did not and does not stop with the lives of the people who have had the privilege of studying in his classes and the many lives touched by them. Dr. Carroll charged him with the responsibility of producing an evangelistic literature. He has written books which have had and are having a wide reading. They have been used of the Holy Spirit to inspire and to instruct many ministers and laymen who never knew the author personally. The titles of his books on evangelism and their copyright dates are as follows: "Recruits for World Conquests" (1914), "With Christ After the Lost" (1919), "Miracles of Divine Leadership" (1920), "Endued to Win" (1922), "The Tears of Jesus" (1922), "Prepare to Meet God" (1922) "Christ's Militant Kingdom" (1924), "Holy Places and Precious Promises" (1924), "A Search for Souls" (1925), "How Jesus Won Men" (1926), "Products of Pentecost" (1924), "Ten Spiritual Ships" (1927), "My Conception of the Gospel Ministry" (1935), "A Blaze of Evangelism Across the Equator" (1937),

4. Scarborough *Op. Cit.* p. 130-131.

and "A Modern School of the Prophets" (1939).[5] This rising tide of vital evangelistic literature will go on influencing men toward Christ and inspiring His witnesses.

In addition to serving the Southwestern Seminary as Professor of Evangelism for thirty-four years, Dr. Scarborough served as president for twenty-seven years. This position gave greater opportunity for his Christ-like passion for men to permeate all the life and work of the school. He has also been a leader in the life and work of his denomination around the world. This leadership has been a potent influence in a generation of vast expansion and accomplishment. His preaching in many revival meetings in all parts of the nation has also been blessed of God in turning thousands to Christ and in building up the churches. In all of this, the pioneer Professor of Evangelism, Seminary President, prolific author, missionary statesman, and general evangelist has found time to seek men personally for Christ. He is still an earnest and an effective personal evangelist.

Dr. Scarborough retired from the Presidency of the Southwestern Seminary in 1942 and was succeeded by Dr. E. D. Head. In harmony with the traditon of the seminary the new president is also Professor of Evangelism. The following courses are listed in the catalog for 1943 and 1944:

"EVANGELISM.

"Courses 1-2. The work of the first year in Evangelism will be a study of the art of soul-winning and personal work using the teacher's book, **With Christ After the Lost,** as a text-book. The text book will be supplemented by lectures and library reading. Two hours per wek throughout the session 1943-44.

"Courses 3-4. The studies for the second year in this department will be a continuation of the studies in Evangelism from the point of view of the soul-winning work of Jesus our saviour. The text-book used is the teacher's **Endued to Win,** which discusses the problem of soul-winning as illustrated in **The Acts of the Apostles** and the missionary program of

5. Dana, *Op. Cit.* p. 86ff.

Paul, showing the methods, principles and plans he used. Two hours per week throughout session 1942-43.

"In connection with these studies the class has large opportunities through the Practical Activities of the Seminary, in winning the lost and in demonstration of the principles and doctrines and methods as taught in the class."[6]

Since the establishment of "The Chair of Fire" in the Southwestern Baptist Theological Seminary in 1908, other seminaries throughout the country have added courses in evangelism to their curricula. All three of the Seminaries of Southern Baptists offer such courses and the majority of Northern Baptists Seminaries do also. Many schools of other evangelical denominations offer regular courses in evangelism at present and a few denominational colleges incorporate it in the regular courses of study.

Just as a Southern Baptist Seminary was the pioneer in teaching evangelism as a regular seminary course, so the Sunday School Board of the Southern Baptist Convention was the pioneer in offering a course in evangelism for Sunday School teachers and officers. The development of the modern Sunday School and its adaptability to evangelistic effort led Southern Baptist leaders to see the need for teacher training in evangelism. Consequently a new book, "Winning to Christ" by P. E. Burroughs, appeared in the teacher training course of Southern Baptists in 1914, the first such book ever to be offered in a teacher training course in the United States.[7] This first book was replaced by another, "How to Win to Christ" by the same author in 1935, but the total number of copies sold was 36,675.

The response of Southern Baptist Sunday School teachers to this training for evangelism and their growing effectiveness in evangelism has led the Sunday School Board to develop an extensive evangelistic literature for teacher training. A total of seven books on evangelism is now offered.

6. Catalog, p. 50.
7. Burroughs, P. E. *Fifty Fruitful Years,* Broadman Press, Nashville, Tennessee. p. 149.

Their titles and copyright dates are as follows: "How to Win to Christ" (1935), "Into All the World" (1935), "Making the World Christian" (1935), "Faith and Its Furtherance" (1936), "The Way Made Plain" (1937), "The Winning Witness" (1938), and "Soul Winning Doctrines" (1943).[8] In addition, a post graduate course is offered which included the following books on evangelism in 1934: "With Christ After the Lost" (Scarborough), and "The Way Made Plain" (Brooks).

During the thirty years that these books have been used a total of 155,245 copies have been sold. This does not include "With Christ After the Lost" which has had a vast circulation. Dr. Burroughs' second book, "How to Win to Christ," has been the best seller, a total of 44,978 copies having been sold since 1935.[9]

These courses in evangelism have been taught in all types of Southern Baptist churches—in country, town and city. They have made a mighty impact upon the evangelization of the South. The revival meeting is more effective in Southern Baptist Churches at present than in any other major denomination of American Christians. The witness of this vast army of men and women is the most potent power in the annual revival and they are making a vital contribution to the ever growing perennial evangelism among Southern Baptists.

But the training of Sunday school teachers is not the only evangelistic training offered to the rank and file of Southern Baptists. Books on Christian witnessing and soul-winning are offered in the Baptist Adult Union training course, the Baptist Young Peoples' Union and the Baptist Intermediate Union.[10] Such books are also offered in the study courses of the Woman's Missionary Union. This training of laymen and women has accelerated the evangelistic advance of Southern Baptists. In the past thirty years,

8. *Ibid.* p. 151.
9. A personal letter from George Card, June 28, 1944.
10. Burroughs, *Op. Cit.* p. 232.

since "Winning to Christ" was first offered to Sunday school teachers. Southern Baptists have grown more rapidly than any other denomination of American Christians.

Some other evangelical denominations have included training for evangelism in their leadership training courses in recent years. The Methodist Episcopal Church began to offer such a course in 1925. The first text book was "Evangelism in the Sunday School" (Chappell). A second book was added in 1940, under the title, "Go ye Therefore" (Brower). The third book, "Evangelism and Christian Education" (Ownbey) was first offered in 1941. A book, "Worship and Evangelism for Youth" is provided for Methodist youth.[11]

The International Council of Religious Education provides the leadership training curricula for most of the evangelical denominations of America. This organization did not provide training for evangelism until 1940. Two text books were presented that year as follows: "Evangelism for Today" (Cartwright), and "The Ministry of Friendly Guidance" (Hoiland). One or the other of these books was taught twenty-nine times in 1941-1942 and twenty-three times in 1942-1943 (The International Council of Religious Education year begins September 1, and closes August 31). The first course in evangelism offered to the large number of churches served by the International Council of Religious Education was reported taught in fifty-two classes during the first two years.

The appearance of training for evangelism in Bible institutes, theological seminaries and colleges presages a better day in evangelistic leadership of the churches. The training of laymen and women in the churches is a token of better things to come because it provides a large group of trained witnesses to support the public proclamation of the evangel and the leadership of the ministers. It also approaches the New Testament teaching that every Christian ought to win others by his personal testimony.

11. A personal letter, July 6, 1944.

CHAPTER XVIII

RADIO EVANGELISM

The appearance of radio as a means of quick direct communication has stirred the imagination and aroused the evangelistic compassion of many Christians. Christian ministers have been preaching the gospel of Christ by this means for nearly a quarter of a century.[1] It is manifestly impossible to know the entire story of radio evangelism for these years because many local stations broadcast religious programs. The number of these stations, and the size and the nature of the audiences, can not be ascertained, but a vast amount of evangelistic preaching has been done over these small local stations. Information is not available as to what percentage of known religious programs are definitely evangelistic, and those who preach the Word in this way have no way of ascertaining the number of conversions which their messages have produced nor the number of lives that have been influenced by them. Enough data are available, however, to reveal a relatively correct estimate of what has been done and what is being done in this new field of evangelistic endeavor.

The First Baptist Church of Shreveport, Louisiana, was the first local church in the United States to own and operate a broadcasting station. Dr. M. E. Dodd, pastor of this church, and his co-workers were and are an evangelistic group. Their zeal for winning others to Christ led them to see the possibilities for evangelism by radio and to establish their own broadcasting station. A contemporary of Dr. Dodd says:

"He is recognized as a great evangelistic preacher, a constructive pastor, a good organizer. and a dynamic Chris-

1. Southern Baptist Home Missions, Aug. 1944, p. 8.

166

tian leader. He has written thirteen books and has contributed much to our religious periodicals. His church was the first in the world to own its own broadcasting station and since 1921 his messages have been broadcast every week."[2] These messages have turned many to Christ who would never have heard the voice of this great evangelistic preacher and dynamic Christian leader but for the radio.

Dr. Ralph W. Sockman, whose voice is often heard on the air, revealed the fact that the imagination of Christian leaders and their evangelistic zeal have been quickened. In a public address in 1938, Dr. Sockman said:

"Some years ago Mr. Louis Broomfield, in his book called 'Possession' made one of his characters, a young man out in Ohio, say something like this—'My grandfathers came into this wilderness to conquer it and subdue it. It was a land filled with savages and adventure. I, too, must have my chance. I am of a race of pioneers, but I have no frontier.'

"That has been somewhat the yeastly feeling of restlessness in the public in recent decades, but we have had the privilege of developing or at least pursuing these great frontiers. We are the spiritual successors of the circuit riders who went shuttling in and out of the mountains like flying shuttles of God, weaving their silken strands of culture into that rough frontier. We go beyond the church wall to those who are sick.

"Mr. Goodman . . . told me some time ago that every day in the city of New York seventy thousand people are taken out of activity by illness. If that ratio holds good over the country something like a million and a half people are ill every day."[3]

Dr. Sockman said that it was these people who do not have the privilege of attending public worship who make up the radio audience. Many others who can not or will not hear

2. *Ibid.*
3. *The Church in the Sky,* Department of National Religious Radio of the Federal Council of The Churches of Christ in America, N. Y., 1938, p. 9-10.

the word in the house of worship are also being reached by radio.

The Department of Religious Radio of the Federal Council of the Churches of Christ in America, with which Dr. Sockman is identifed, began broadcasting religious programs over the facilities of the Natonal Broadcasting Company on May 23, 1923. During the next fifteen years they sent more than six thousand programs over the air. The response to these programs has been vast. More than seven million comments from all of the forty-eight states were received in fifteen years.

The facilities of the National Broadcasting Company were donated to the Federal Council's Department of National Religious Radio. The time used by these religious broadcasts could have been sold by the company for a million dollars per year. A majority of these programs have not been definitely evangelistic but they have contributed to the evangelistic accomplishments of the churches of America.

The Moody Bible Institute of Chicago entered the field of radio evangelism in 1925, two years after the first broadcast by the Federal Council on a nation-wide hook-up. The complete story of this evangelistic program was furnished by the Moody Bible Institute in August, 1944. It follows:

"In 1925, the Moody Bible Institute of Chicago, by God's providence, was led into the field of radio. The Institute had been invited along with other Chicago organizations to have a booth at an exposition. The school intended to interest folk who came to visit the exposition in the Institute's ministry, and also to present a gospel testimony through the distribution of tracts. To attract attenion, two students stood outside the booth and played cornets.

"Across the aisle was an exhibit by station WGES, which periodically through the day broadcast from the exposition. They invited the cornetists to play on one of their programs. Then they offered free time to the Institute on Sunday, which was gladly accepted from October, 1925, through February, 1926.

"The value of this new field for spreading the gospel was quickly recognized, and six hours a week were purchased for a time, then increased to nine hours, over the same station. On March 3, 1926, a regular fourteen and one-half hour schedule over WENR was begun.

"A license was obtained from the government on July 28, 1926, and from the two towers on top of the Women's Building, with a 500-watt transmitter, the Institute began broad-casting with its own call letters, WMBI.

"In 1928, a modern transmitting plant was built at Addison, Illinois, about twenty miles west of Chicago, using 5000 watts as power. In 1938 a new 490-foot vertical radiator was erected, which greatly increased the efficiency and range, although it is possible with daytime broadcasting to cover a radius of about 300 miles, depending on weather conditions. For a time, a midnight hour was broadcast, which could be heard in all the United States, and reports were received from remote lands and islands. Fiji Islanders were among the regular listeners, as well as inhabitants of the Hawaiian Islands, Central and South America, Alaska, Cuba, Puerto Rico and New Zealand.

"On March 4, 1941, the Federal Communications Commission granted the Institute permission to construct a frequency modulation station. This was one of five FM transmitters in the Chicago area.

"After an extensive period of experimental broadcasting, the Institute's FM station, at first called W75C, now WDLM, received its provisional license in April, 1943. Dedication of the station did not take place, however, until November 1, 1943.

"The frequency modulation antenna is installed atop the 490-foot transmitter of its sister station WMBI. While WDLM has been granted permission to construct a 50,000-watt transmitter, it is operating for the duration of the war on 1,000 watts, because of the scarcity of materials. WDLM is the first station in the Chicago area to use an ultra high frequency modulation FM transmitter, which beams the programs from its Chicago studios to the transmitter at Addison, Illinois.

"During its eighteen years of broadcasting WMBI and more recently WDLM have aimed at variety of presentation while following the unity of the gospel message. Unlike commercial stations, which have a wide range of subjects from which to choose, an almost inexhaustible source of material on which to draw, with high-salaried continuity writers and many officials, as well as an unlimited supply of talent, the Moody Bible Institute must throughout its twelve hours (more in the summer, less in the winter) of broadcasting each day stay close to the general theme of religion, as it is classified by radio authority.

"While WMBI has a regular broadcasting license and is in the commercial band, it has never sold any time. This is the station dedicated wholly to the service of our Lord and Saviour Jesus Christ, carved on the cornerstone of the transmitting plant, is the slogan of WMBI and WDLM, which characterizes the programs. No commercial announcement has ever gone out over the stations; no jazz has been sent out on the air waves; no cigarette or liquor business has been advanced through these facilties.

"A summary of the programs aired by the Institute stations reveals a wide variety—Bible study, sermons, inspirational thoughts, sketches, stories, educational features, and news, with a high percentage of vocal and instrumental music. Special programs are planned for children, young people and shut-ins. In addition, classes in Radio School of the Bible are taught five days a week by faculty and staff instructors. During the years there have been actual registrations in the Radio School of more than 20,000 persons.

"Other Bible periods include the International Sunday School Lesson; Golden Nuggets—Greek word studies; Old Testament stories. The morning service of one of Chicago's churches is broadcast every Sunday, each church broadcasting for a period of two months. Living up to their interdenominational character, the radio stations have broadcast services from Presbyterian, Evangelical Mission Covenant, Baptist, Evangelical Free, Christian and Missionary Alliance, and independent churches.

"Early each morning, Sunrise Songs give the time, temperature, gospel music and news. No. 9, Elm Street is a popular serial sketch. Another favorite program is Continued Story Reading.

"Missionary information and challenge are presented regularly, in World-Wide Missions and Missionary Sketch. Your Church School and Home Hour are also featured each week.

"Gospel songs and hymns, sacred classics and choir music, together with organ, novachord, piano, orchestra and other instrumental contributions are provided in such programs as Hymn Sing, Hymns for the Home, Morning Melodies, Solo Time, Evensong, Girl's Glee Club, Brass Quartet, Singing Strings, Voice of the Novachord, Master Works of Music, Piano Classics.

"There are other special features, such as Child Evangelism; KYB Club (Know Your Bible Club), a children's gospel variety program; Teen-Age Bible Study; Young People's Hour.

"Before the war WMBI had a special appeal to foreign language groups. Regular weekly broadcasts were given in Swedish, Norwegian, German, Hebrew, Russian, Greek, Italian, Mexican, Bohemian and other native tongues.

"A large percentage of the programs are of a spiritual nature, as will be seen from the following table, compiled from the radio log for a month:

Religious	66	per cent
Entertainment	20	
Educational	6	1/3
News	6	
Governmental	1	
Agricultural		1/3
Civic		1/3

The station's equipment includes studios in the Administration Building. These are of latest design and modern in every respect, with visitors' balconies. Two of the studios will each hold one hundred people. In the mechanical end RCA and Western Electric equipment is used, including transcription facilities for both making and broadcasting this type of program. The operators are licensed by the United States Government. All of the announcers, singers, speakers, operators, mechanics, and members of the radio staff are consecrated Christians.

"The singing ensembles, chosen from the advanced music students of the Institute, are moderately paid for their work, as well as student announcers, continuity writers, and incidental helpers. Thus many of them are able to continue in school with this financial assistance. An efficient staff of full-time workers is maintained for the answering of hundreds of pieces of mail weekly, and for training groups for the broadcasts, as well as planning program production.

"Keeping abreast of the times, and the particular needs of the churches, the Moody Bible Institute offers an elective course in Radio Broadcasting, which includes the history, the mechanics, the psychology of radio, and the production of programs and preparation of material; transcriptions, newspaper publicity, network broadcasting and Bible reading.

"Another outgrowth of the Institute's radio ministry is 'Miracles of Melodies.' Following a survey of 271 station managers, seven series of thirteen fifteen-minute transcribed programs were prepared and offered to radio stations willing to accept them on a sustaining basis. These programs consist of singing and playing of old hymns and gospel songs, and the re-enactment of a true story in which the faith of devout men and women perform a 'modern miracle.'

"These transcriptions have been used by more than 300 radio stations, in 35 states, Canada, China, Puerto Rico, Hawaii, South America, Alaska and North Africa. Recently the transcriptions have been used by chaplains, not only here in training centers, but aboard the troop transports, battle-ships, and even in the huge bombers as they soar forth to battle. An army chaplain of North Africa writes: 'One of your transcriptions is broadcast each Sunday evening over the army radio station, reaching all of North Africa and part of the continent of Europe.'

"As a part of the Moody Bible Institute, the radio stations are supported, as is the whole Institute, by voluntary gifts from friends interested in its ministry. WMBI and WDLM never make frantic appeals for money on their programs. Rarely have more than two minutes been used for an announcement of a financial nature, and the phrase characterizing most of these announcements is, 'These programs are kept on the air from funds sent in by interested listeners.'

"The Moody Bible Institute, not only in the Radio Department, but in all of its work, treats as a sacred trust the money received. Full accounting is given. All accounts are audited. All work is supervised carefully by a board of trustees of representative business men and an executive committee which meets with the president each week. Salaries are modest. The work is planned with a view to the widest possible presentation of the gospel message and the dissemination of the Word of God with the least financial appeal possible."

This detailed account of one of the most effective evangelistic programs now being offered to the American public reveals a variety of material with the evangelistic message as the chief emphasis. Many thousands of people have heard and are hearing the gospel over the Moody stations.

The beginnings of the Old Fashioned Revival Hour appeared in 1928. It was inaugurated because Rev. Charles E. Fuller was led by the Holy Spirit to see the vast possibilites of evangelism by radio. His first broadcast was from Indianapolis, Indiana, in 1927, when he was asked to speak as a substitute for the regular speaker. His fifteen minute message was received very enthusiastically and his interest in this new means for spreading the gospel was quickened[4] In February, 1928, he arranged to broadcast his Sunday services from Calvary Church of Placentia, California, over station KGER of Long Beach, California.[5] He soon added a Thursday evening Bible Hour which also proved to be an effective evangelistic broadcast. He continued to broadcast from Calvary Church for five years before giving up the pastorate to give all his time to evangelism by means of the radio.

In 1933, Mr. Fuller organized the Gospel Broadcasting Association to look after the financial needs of his radio ministry.[6] Four years later the facilities of the Mutual Broadcasting System were secured to send out the Old Fashioned Revival Hour from coast to coast. This is one of the most popular radio broadcasts on the air today. Mr. Fuller makes no effort to keep a record of the number of conversions which his radio ministry produces. He modestly declines to give an estimate, but his gospel messages are heard all over America and beyond our borders. Many thousands have been brought to Christ and myriads of lives have been blessed by the Old Fashioned Revival Hour.

Rev. Percy B. Crawford inaugurated the Young People's Church of the Air in Philadelphia, Pennsylvania, in 1931. At present there are eight broadcasts per week. The Sunday sermons are definitely evangelistic and an appeal is made at the close of each sermon for people to receive Christ as Lord and Saviour. Mr. Crawford estimates that from five to ten thousand persons are converted annually through the influence of the Young Peoples' Church of the Air.[7]

One of the most potent evangelistic broadcasts now on the air is the International Lutheran Hour with its motto, "Bringing Christ to the Nations." This ministry was inaugurated in 1935 by Dr. Walter A. Maier, a professor in

4. *Ibid.* p. 30.
5. Wright, J. Elvin, *The Old Fashioned Revival Hour and the Broadcasters,* The Fellowship Press, Boston, 1942, p. 24.
6. *Ibid.* p. 91-92.
7. A personal letter from Mr. Crawford, Aug. 1944.

Concordia Seminary of Saint Louis, Missouri. He was given financial support by Mr. William S. Knudson.

Dr. Maier's first message was broadcast by a Detroit station, but nine years later his regular broadcasts were being carried by two hundred twenty-four stations in the United States over the Mutual Broadcasting System. More than three hundred and fifty other local stations were releasing these messages by transcription. It is estimated that fifteen million people in twenty-six countries hear these burning gospel messages each week at present. The total expense of broadcasting the Lutheran Hour is now a half million dollars annually and it is paid by voluntary contributions from the vast radio audience.[8]

The gospel messages proclaimed to the nations by Dr. Maier are evangelical in doctrine and evangelistic in spirit and motive. He preaches that men are lost in sin and that they can find salvation only through faith in Christ. Many have found salvation from sin because of these positive messages. Only isolated examples of these evangelistic results are available, but they indicate a wide-spread response. For example, a Negro woman in Pittsburgh, Pennsylvania, heard his messages and became interested. She wrote to Dr. Maier that she desired to have her children baptized. A Lutheran minister called in the home, others became interested and a Negro church was organized with two hundred members.

The gospel is going out over the air from many voices not mentioned in this chapter. It is reaching many thousands of people and is turning many to Christ. A survey made in 1942 of programs in the Chicago area revealed that the majority of the relogous programs were definitely evangelical and evangelistic.[9] Eternity alone can reveal the results. It is likely that this new method in evangelism will be used more and more in the future.

8. Collier's Magazine, Issue of May 4, 1944.
9. The Chicago Theological Seminary Register. Issue of January, 1942.

CHAPTER XIX

WHITHER EVANGELISM?

Evangelism is primarily a work of God and not of men. The leaders in evangelism must constantly remember that it is not by might nor by power nor by techniques but by the Spirit of God that individuals and human society are to be redeemed. God is doing His work of redemption, however, in the frame-work of human history and through human agencies. Some one has well said that a wise man seeks to find out which way God is going and to go with Him. The way He is going in vital transforming evangelism is revealed with some clarity by the way He has been going through American history since the founding of the Jamestown Colony in 1607.

This final chapter is an effort to understand and to evaluate the evangelism of today in the light of its history. It is also an effort to discover how Christ's witnesses may best be "laborers together with God" in presenting the saving Gospel to this generation. It is manifestly impossible to understand the evangelism of today and the probable trends of tomorrow without the historical perspective. The historical developments which have helped to mould the evangelism of today reveal some logical ways to approach the present generation and to go on with God in His work of redemption.

The tides of vital evangelism have ebbed and flowed in American life. The low tide has always come in time of war and during the periods of reconstruction and adjustment which have followed the wars of American history. Infidelity has always thrived and morals have become exceedingly corrupt in the times of low tide. The dark days of the first quarter of the eighteenth century in Colonial America followed the inter-colonial wars. The hey-day of French Deism and its accompanying gross immorality was the fifteen years after the American Revolution. The Civil War was followed by a period of corruption in government, race and class hatred and other forms of vice. The crime wave, crass materialism and godlessness which swept America after the first World War bears consistent testimony to the fact that war stifles evangelism and immorality flourishes when evangelism is stifled.

The dark and difficult days of low tide have been swept away by a rising tide of vital evangelism. Three times in the life of the nation infidelity has been routed and moral conditions have been vastly improved by a period of revival. It was through the Great Awakening that the darkness of the first quarter of the eighteenth century was dispelled. It was through countless local revivals along the eastern seaboard, the mighty awakenings in the colleges of that area and the famous camp meetings of the frontier that French Deism was successfully challenged and moral standards were raised. It was also during the early years of this period of revival that home and foreign mission enterprises came into being. The religious press of America was born in this era of spiritual awakening and Christian education received a new impetus. The ratio of church members to the total population was raised from 5% in 1790 to 22.7% in 1860. The great tabernacle revivals appeared after the Civil War to turn thousands to Christ and to inaugurate and support many social reforms. These were supplemented by many local revivals, special work among the socially under-privileged and the rise of educational evangelism. Youth movements in evangelism also made great contributions to the evangelistic advance which brought the ratio of church membership to the total population from 17.5% in 1870 to 34.4% in 1910—the last statistics available before the outbreak of the first World War. This rising tide of vital religion raised moral standards and contributed to many moral reforms such as National Prohibition.

The time between the first World War and the present global conflict was too short for an awakening to appear and its fruits to be evaluated. The ratio of church members to the total population which was 34.4% in 1920 as it had been in 1910 increased to 50.3% in 1942 despite the fact that the tabernacle revival has disappeared and the local revival seems to be losing its potency in many sections. There were some evidences of the coming of an awakening during the last few years prior to Hitler's invasion of Poland which plunged the world into the present gruesome struggle. The number of church members continued to increase up to 1942 but the moral reformation which accompanies a vital religious awakening was not evident. The standards of church membership have been lowered and many are enrolled as church members who show no evidence of a vital religious experience. This appears in low moral standards which permitted the repeal of the National Prohibition Act and in the additional fact that fewer than 40% of the members of the evangelical churches of America are enlisted in the service of Christ and humanity through the churches.

The wars which have plagued our country have been local wars—confined to this country. The first World War is an exception but the era since its close is too short for an historical analysis. The spiritual awakenings which have brought such rich blessings to the nation have also been local—confined to the United States. The world is now engulfed in a colossal war in which nearly all the nations of the earth are involved. May we not, therefore, pray for and confidently expect a world-wide spiritual awakening when the peoples of the earth have recovered somewhat from the shock of a total global war? The thinking and the planning of many religious leaders around the world seem to indicate that the Spirit of God is moving upon the Christian people of America to such an awakening. This is the way God seems to be going through the turmoil of current history.

It seems that the evangelism of today and tomorrow will be based upon a sound educational procedure. An understanding of the psychology of religious experience will enable the Christian worker to present his appeal to the total personality, and not primarily to the emotional nature. The development of the programs of religious education in most of the evangelical churches has also laid solid foundations for this technique in evangelism. The early teaching of the child prepares for the conversion experience by teaching fundamental religious truths. The teaching subsequent to the conversion experience interprets that experience and leads to growth. The expressional activities provided for the new convert by his church also deepen the impressions of truth and must not ignore the work of the Holy Spirit or the necessity of the new birth. The Holy Spirit approaches the human personality, however, in His work of calling, convicting of sin and regeneration. The reactions of the human personality in a crisis can be analyzed and understood psychologically. The conversion experience may, therefore, be prepared for, interpreted and brought to fruition through sound educational processes under the leadership of the Holy Spirit.

The study of the psychology of religion did not appear until near the beginning of the twentieth century but the educational foundation of the Great Awakening in Colonial America was laid upon solid psychological bases. The public school curriculum was entirely religious in content and in purpose. The textbooks were the Bible, the Horn Book, the Psalter and the Westminster Catechism. All the Bible material was interpreted in the light of Calvinistic theology. When the preachers of Great Awakening fame addressed the people, they used the very language and thought forms of the public schools. To a people thus educationally prepared and thus addressed with the gospel message, the Holy Spirit came in power and the period of revival which history has named the Great Awakening swept the country. Many thousands were converted, moral standards were raised and the stamina which was necessary to win the war for independence was created. The complete secularization of the public school curriculum was not finished until near the outbreak of the Civil War. The leaders in evangelism from the Revolution to the Civil War were also speaking to a people who were steeped in theology, Scripture and the language of the Bible.

The educational foundations of the two great periods of

religious awakenings contrasted with the public school curriculum of the present raise certain disturbing and challenging
questions for the leader in evangelism today and tomorrow.
The curriculum is entirely secular and largely materialistic.
The religious motive is absent and Bible material does not appear at all. People have been taught from childhood that
they may find the abundant life in material things, the products of modern materalistic science. The motive for getting
an education has been the making of money primarily. Instead of the abundant life, however, we have abundant death.
The flower of the world's young manhood is being slaughter-
ed by the inventions of modern materialistic scientists. May
not our Lord's witnesses say to this generation, You have
abundant death now because Christ has not been Lord of material things and of the men who handle them? Is it not rea-
sonable to believe that the preaching and the teaching of
Christian stewardship may be the foundation for the next
great spiritual awakening? It is imperative that materialistic education be brought under the authority of Christ. Otherwise, the prospect is that the human race may literally com-
mit suicide. Will the Christian leaders of today and tomorrow
have the wisdom and the training to capture the results of
modern science for Christ and to dedicate them to the good of
humanity? The emergence of Christian stewardship in the
thinking of American Christians is a hopeful sign. The evangelist who would present Christ to the modern mind which is
so full of materialism and selfish motives will need the widest
and most thorough training possible. He can no longer be a
man of one book even if that book is the Bible, the eternal
Word of God. He will need to understand all the thought cur-
rents of his day if he is to wield the Sword of the Spirit in a
battle that is influenced by so many forces.

Many other facts of current history indicate that the
evangelism of today and tomorrow will be largely the winning of men day by day rather than at special seasons and by
special efforts. Special seasons and meetings will continue to
be used but the churches will depend upon them less and less
for evangelistic results. The great tabernacle meeting has
recently disappeared as did the famous "Camp Meetings" of

an earlier generation. It may return but at present it does not so appear. The local revival seems to be waning in effectiveness but an increasing number of churches are witnessing conversions week by week in the regular services of worship. The increasing numbers of laymen who have had some training in evangelism are doing effective work and the number of church members in America continued to increase up to 1942. It was during that year that the ratio of church membership increased to 50%. It was the first time in the history of the United States that more than fifty per cent of the people were church members. The changing of methods and the development of new techniques does not necessarily mean that evangelism is either waxing or waning. Christ is the same yesterday and today and forever but He must be presented to each succeeding generation by methods that are psychologically sound and adapted to current conditions. The Christian witness must not be too trammeled by tradition.

If the major part of the evangelizing of America is to be done through the regular work of the churches and if the daily witnessing of laymen is to play an important role in it, the training of personal evangelists in the churches must be vastly more extensive and thorough than it is at present. A survey revealed a few years ago that only five per cent of the membership of one great evangelistic denomination in America ever attempted to win some one to Christ by personal effort. This will necessitate more evangelistc training for pastors in the colleges and seminaries of America. The pastor moulds the leadership training of the church he serves. If training in evangelism is to have its rightful place the pastor must be imbued with a Christ-like passion to win men. He must be able to say as Paul said, "I could wish that I myself were anathema from Christ for others." He must know also the very best methods for his own generation. The work of evangelism is too vitally important for time and for eternity to be done half-heartedly or by inferior or out-moded techniques. If the pastor is to bear the cross for a lost world and to know the best methods for his generation, his seminary must bear the burden of the lost world and must teach him how to take men alive by the most skilful methods. This was the method of the Master who trained the first fishers of men. Every department of instruction in the seminary and every phase of its life must be imbued with the evangelistic passion and the courses offered in evangelism must be constantly enlarged and improved to meet the needs of a constantly changing world.

The winning of the unchurched masses of America is perhaps the greatest task of evangelism today. This can be done most effectively and constructively through the growing of churches whose members have both the desire and the skill to go out into the highways and by-ways and constrain them to come in. There may be a place for special efforts and methods to present Christ to the socially underprivileged but that can be done best under the supervision of great evangelistic churches. If mission Sunday schools are to be established and mission revivals are to be held, these can best be done under the supervision of established churches with a Christlike passion for the underprivileged.

Some leaders in American Christendom have become so alarmed over the low moral standards of church members and the impotency of so many churches in their witness to a lost world that they are insisting upon a vital personal religous experience. This is a good omen. The passion for adding names to the church rolls which seized so many evangelists and other Christian leaders a few years ago has brought many unregenerate persons into the membership of the churches. It is to be feared that this condition will stifle evangelism in our day very much as did the Half-way Covenant and Birthright Membership in early Colonial times. This is one of the gravest perils to the evangelism of today and tomorrow.

The world of today calls in no uncertain terms for an evangelism which will produce social and economic adjustments upon Christian principles. Such adjustments will be made only through the leavening influence of men and women who have become new creatures in Christ Jesus. The evangelism of the past has been too willing to stop at the new birth but in so far as it has insisted upon and produced twice-born men it has been wise. It has shown lack of wisdom in failing to go on "perfecting the saints" both individually and in the group. It has largely missed the mind of the Master that the Kingdom of God means a new human society in this world in which dwelleth righteousness. It is of urgent importance that men be saved from the ultimate consequences of sin and for eternity. It is of more urgent importance now than ever before in the world's history that men be redeemed to function in leavening the entire structure of human society. The world has become a small neighborhood through the amazing accomplishments of modern science. The clash of nations and of races which were formerly isolated is now shaking the very foundations of a civilization based upon non-Christian principles. The clash of greedy economic interests is at the very foundation of the clash of nations and of racial groups. For the social and economic world of today and tomorrow the witness for Christ must see and speak the truth that, "Other foundation can no man lay than that which is laid, which is Jesus Christ."

Methods and techniques for making Christ Lord of all life that He may take away the clash and clang of races and nations are yet to be developed. There are some grave dangers in present trends. The greatest danger lies in shallow thinking that men may fit into a Christan social order who are not themselves Christians. Unregenerate men are not stable foundation stones for the new structure. Another peril is that Christians and Christian leaders may lose sight of the individual in an effort to deal with men en masse. A prominent leader said recently that there is very little conviction for personal sin in the society of today but that there is much conviction for corporate sin. Men as individuals are not directly responsible for much of the evil of our time. This leader concludes that preachers ought to condemn the sins of groups—the capitalists or the labor organizations or the political parties. This is true but our Lord's witnesses must never forget that men as individuals are sinners against God and must repent and believe individually. It is well to condemn corporate sin but it must be remembered that corporate sin is but the sum of the sins of all the members of the group. One may preach about the sins of capitalism with earnestness and convincing logic but no capitalist will repent until he faces the fact that the sin of his own life is the root of the whole matter. No laborer will be called to repentance by a condemnation of the sins of the labor movement and no politician will humble himself before God and receive the new birth just because some one reminds him of the sins of the party. The fact of so-called corporate sin is a good foundation for revealing the sins of individuals and their consequences in the life of the nation but the evangelist must never lose sight of the individual and of his personal need of redemption.

It seems likely that the radio will be used with increasing effectiveness in the evangelism of tomorrow. The developments in that field are of course unpredictable. The progress made, however, seems to indicate that this miracle of modern scientific thinking will be an effective instrument in the hands of the evangelist of tomorrow.

Many phases of the history of the United States indicate that it is the purpose of God to use our nation to evangelize the world. It seems that America has been providentially prepared and placed in a position of leadership among the nations for this very purpose. The home and foreign mission enterprises in our country came into being shortly after the beginnings of the second awakening. The first home mission society in America was organized nine years after the appearance of the local revivals which swept French Deism from the life of the nation and greatly improved the morals of the nation. The first foreign mission board was organized nineteen years after the beginnings of those revivals and ten years after the awakenings began in the colleges. American Christendom would not have responded to the call of the world need but for the tidal wave of vital evangelism which prepared for it. Since American Christians began to share in this world-wide movement to win all men for Christ there has been more effective evangelism at home. If it is in the providence of God to use our nation as a leader in winning the whole world to Christ, the most urgent need is a great spiritual awakening in our own land. The need is for an awakening that will make individuals to be new creatures in Christ Jesus and lead them to leaven the whole lump of human society. There are evidences even in the present tragic struggle among the nations that the Spirit of God is leading to such a revival. The way in which this visitation of God's mercy and power may come to our land is in His own hands. Those of us who long for it as a watchman longs for the morning may be more effective "laborers together with God" in bringing it about if we remember that it is not by might nor by power but by His Spirit. We may also be able to catch step with the eternal God as he moves on in the history of our nation by a knowledge of the history of evangelism from the planting of the first colony to the present hour.

INDEX